Emotional Intelligence (EQ)

A Leadership Imperative!

Daire Coffey &
Deirdre Murray

MANAGEMENT BRIEFS

Essential Insights for Busy Managers

© 2010 by Daire Coffey and Deirdre Murray
First published in 2010. Reprinted 2011.
ISBN 978-1-906946-06-7

Production credits
All design, artwork and liaison with printers has been undertaken by Neworld Associates,
9 Greenmount Avenue, Harold's Cross, Dublin 12, www.neworld.com

Publisher: Management Briefs, 30 The Palms, Clonskeagh, Dublin 14.

Table of Contents

Acknowledgements

They say learning is a 'journey rather than a destination' and that certainly is the case with this book! We would like to extend our sincere thanks to all the leaders out there who have inspired us to embark on this journey. Also, to clients, colleagues, mentors and friends from whom we have learned so much.

We especially would like to thank Frank Scott-Lennon for his endless encouragement and advice. We are very grateful to clients, colleagues and mentors for their insightful suggestions as well as those who patiently read the final drafts! In particular, we extend our thanks to the following: Dr. Simon Boucher, Joan Bree, John Broderick, Caroline Casey, Mary Collins, Aidan Connolly, Frances Keane, Dr. Phillip Matthews, Andrew McLoughlin, Enda McNulty, Liz Norris, Mary O'Shaughnessy, Fiona O'Sullivan, James Sweetman, Greg Swift and Alistair Tosh.

We are indebted to Dr. Martyn Newman of RocheMartin, a leading authority in this area and author of 'Emotional Capitalists - The New Leaders,' who has personally inspired us to further elevate the importance of EQ in the leadership arena.

Lastly, we cannot forget our husbands, Mick and David, as well as our families and friends for their endless patience and support.
Enjoy...

Daire Coffey and Deirdre Murray

November 2010

Foreword

How do the world's most effective leaders make it to the top and stay there? Experience, technical skills and business acumen are not enough in themselves. The most influential leaders know how to engage the real drivers of effective performance - emotions.

Emotions really are the engine in the vehicle of leadership performance, and the skills associated with using emotions intelligently are indispensable to achieving outstanding success. In this book, Daire and Deirdre provide a wealth of practical strategies for systematically building the skills of emotional intelligence to achieve remarkable leadership influence. Quite simply, this book tells you how to do it - it is an intensely practical guide to interpreting and acquiring the skills of emotional intelligence that support leadership excellence.

Building on the solid research-based foundation of the Emotional Capital Model, it has become very clear that the skills that separate average leaders from star performers are grounded in the ability to manage one's own emotions well and effectively engage the emotions of others.

I wholeheartedly recommend this book as it is informative, packed with psychological insights and techniques and is entertaining. Read it today, commit to the ideas and practise the skills. The authors have given us an important back stage pass for taking personal and professional performance to new levels of achievement.

Martyn Newman, PhD, DPsych
MD, RocheMartin
Author, Emotional Capitalists: The New Leaders
Melbourne, Australia

June 2010

Section I
Introduction to the Concept of EQ

What is Emotional Intelligence (EQ) and Why Does it Matter?

1

Chapter outline
What is Emotional Intelligence (EQ) and Why Does it Matter?

"No doubt emotional intelligence is more rare than book smarts. But my experience says it is actually more important in the making of a leader."

Jack Welch, former CEO General Electric

→ So What is Emotional Intelligence (EQ)?
→ EQ is Not a New Concept
→ Why EQ Matters More Than Ever
→ EQ and IQ Complement Each Other
→ Dispelling the Myths about EQ
→ EQ Can be Learned and Developed!

Introduction

In this chapter, we define Emotional Intelligence (EQ), how it complements IQ and why it is a critical leadership skill set for achieving success in today's challenging environment. We also learn that, with practice, it can be learned and developed!

So What is Emotional Intelligence (EQ)?

Why is it that two people with the same level of IQ can go on to achieve very different levels of success in life? We now know that IQ alone is not enough and that there exists a set of non-cognitive competencies that determine people's ability to achieve success. This other kind of 'smart' is referred to as Emotional Intelligence, hereinafter referred to as EQ.

"EQ is about being 'smart' with your emotions... it's about tuning in to yourself and others and then using this valuable information to better manage yourself and your relationships with others."

Coffey and Murray

EQ

'The difference that makes the difference!'

'Advanced commonsense'

'Smart' with emotions!

'Being rounded and balanced'

According to a survey undertaken by the Gallup Organisation, the No. 1 reason why people stay and thrive in an organisation is because of their immediate boss. Unfortunately, it is also the No.1 reason why people leave. So much money is spent trying to retain top talent through pay incentives, perks and training, when in the end, turnover is mainly a management issue. While many leaders may have strong technical 'know-how' and business acumen, if they lack the ability to communicate and inspire others, they will be unable to drive performance and achieve better results.

"People leave managers, not companies"

Buckingham and Coffman, The Gallup Organisation

Think of a great boss with whom you worked in the past. What characteristics and competencies come to mind when you think of him/her? Was it IQ, education, technical know-how that made them stand out? Then think of a boss who was completely ineffective. What characteristics did he/she have?

Think of the 'best' and the 'worst' boss you ever had...

Describe on the following page the behaviours they typically demonstrated:

'Best' Boss

_____

_____

_____

_____

_____

_____

_____

'Worst' Boss

_____

_____

_____

_____

_____

_____

_____

You will probably find that the characteristics and competencies of the best leaders tend to relate to their high EQ, rather than their IQ! Similarly, the characteristics and competencies of ineffective leaders tend to relate to their lack of EQ! The general descriptors associated with the best and worst bosses are outlined below:

'Best' Boss

'Had a clear vision'

'Listened to me'

'Brought the best out in me and others'

'Was resilient'

'Was an excellent communicator'

'Was approachable'

'Had good judgment'

'Remained calm under pressure'

HIGH EQ

'Worst' Boss

'Didn't listen'

'Was bad-tempered'

'Poor communicator'

'Tactless'

'Rigid in his/her ideas'

'Couldn't make decisions'

'Was critical of me'

'Held grudges'

LOW EQ

EQ is Not a New Concept

Psychologists have been trying to define intelligence for many years. For the past century, intelligence has been measured with IQ, which relates to cognitive intelligence, i.e. our ability to learn, recall and apply logical reasoning. An outline of the history and development of the concept of EQ is shown below:

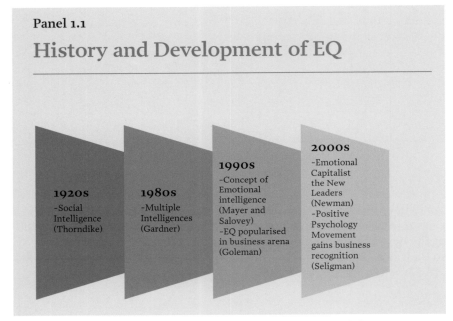

Panel 1.1

History and Development of EQ

1920S
-Social Intelligence (Thorndike)

1980s
-Multiple Intelligences (Gardner)

1990s
-Concept of Emotional intelligence (Mayer and Salovey)
-EQ popularised in business arena (Goleman)

2000s
-Emotional Capitalist the New Leaders (Newman)
-Positive Psychology Movement gains business recognition (Seligman)

In the 1920s, Thorndike put forward the idea that there was a 'social intelligence' but did not have empirical research to back up this concept. In the 1980s, Harvard psychologist Gardner developed this further with the concept of 'multiple intelligences,' which included both intrapersonal and interpersonal skills. The term 'emotional intelligence' was initially introduced by Mayer and Salovey in the 1990s and was further popularised by Goleman in 1995, in his best-selling book, 'Emotional Intelligence - *Why It Can Matter More Than IQ.*'

Goleman examined the concept of how two people with the same IQ, could achieve vastly different levels of success in their professional and personal lives. His book received critical acclaim and along with significant advances in the neuroscience arena, put the concept of EQ firmly on the business agenda, once and for all.

More recently, Martyn Newman has conducted empirical research specifically in the leadership arena. His research concluded that leaders who instilled *"energy, enthusiasm and commitment in the hearts of everyone connected with the business,"* had a competitive advantage in achieving improved performance and better results. He refers to these leaders as 'Emotional Capitalists™.' These leaders exemplify a set of emotional and social skills that are most effective in influencing others.

Research undertaken by Martin Seligman into the concept of *"learned optimism"* is one of the key tenets of EQ. His studies have shown that those who display a realistic sense of optimism tend to be much more successful in their professional and personal lives.

The theory behind EQ is outlined in the model below:

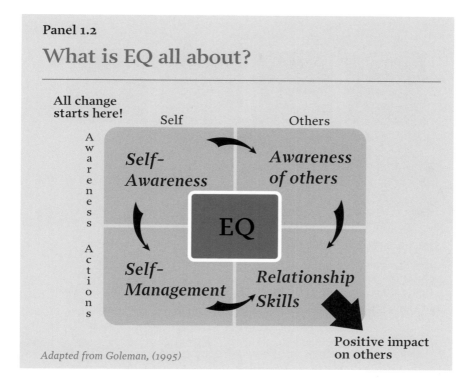

Panel 1.2

What is EQ all about?

Adapted from Goleman, (1995)

EQ Explained:

Goleman states that all emotional intelligence starts with self. EQ success is about initially developing self-awareness and management of our emotions. Once we have mastered this, we can then learn to develop our awareness of the emotions and feelings of others and use this information to adopt more appropriate behaviours. This ultimately leads to improved relationships with others.

Adopting the TACT© Approach

TACT© provides you with four easy steps to develop your EQ.

We recommend that you use the TACT© approach throughout the book to improve your personal and interpersonal effectiveness.

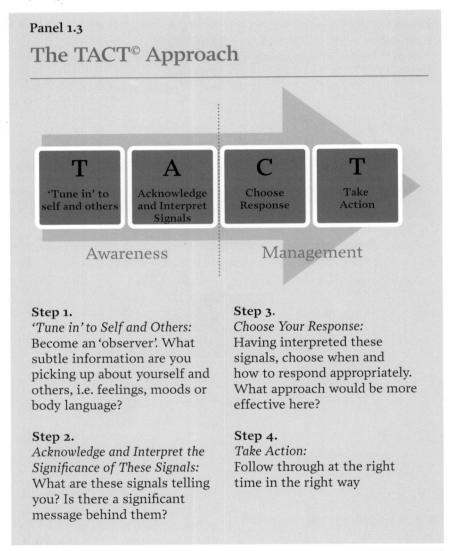

Panel 1.3

The TACT© Approach

T	**A**	**C**	**T**
'Tune in' to self and others	Acknowledge and Interpret Signals	Choose Response	Take Action

Awareness | Management

Step 1.
'Tune in' to Self and Others:
Become an 'observer'. What subtle information are you picking up about yourself and others, i.e. feelings, moods or body language?

Step 2.
Acknowledge and Interpret the Significance of These Signals:
What are these signals telling you? Is there a significant message behind them?

Step 3.
Choose Your Response:
Having interpreted these signals, choose when and how to respond appropriately. What approach would be more effective here?

Step 4.
Take Action:
Follow through at the right time in the right way

Remember, in any situation, it is important to use the TACT© Approach to enhance your EQ!

Why EQ Matters More Than Ever

*"The lack of EQ is the No. 1 derailing factor for leaders."
(Center for Creative Leadership)*

The workplace is in a constant state of flux with many challenges. Leaders are facing increasing pressures and have to consistently do more with less. People are not only required to work harder but also smarter.

Competition is on the increase, and product lifecycles are getting shorter. While advanced technology can facilitate our productivity, it also means we are constantly 'on call' 24/7 with our Blackberries and mobile phones.

Panel 1.4

Increasing Demands and Pressures

With increasing demands placed upon us, the ability to manage ourselves and our relationships with others is **more critical than ever:**

→ There is a shift away from 'command and control' style to one that empowers and inspires

→ People now aspire to follow leaders who not only have a clear strategy but who also share a compelling vision that engages both the heart and head

→ EQ is as important, if not more important than IQ, particularly in leadership roles.

The Business Case for EQ:

In today's business world, the emphasis is often on daring strategies and technical competence. However, while this is important it is no longer enough. Too many companies have floundered by concentrating solely on short-term financial gains.

As Herb Kelleher, former CEO of Southwest Airlines once said, *"the business of business is people."* Kelleher always operated on the premise of putting people first, through his philosophy of the three P's: *"people, performance, profit."* Development of your EQ is not an expense but an investment that pays off in the longer term.

Developing EQ among business leaders in your organisation can bring lasting benefits by creating new levels of peak performance for you, your team and the entire organisation. The increasing importance of EQ as a key success factor in leadership is now supported by empirical research. Studies over a range of business enterprises reinforce the **business case for EQ** in leadership:

→ The US Air Force found that their most successful recruiters scored significantly higher in EQ competencies of Assertiveness, Empathy, Happiness and Self Awareness

→ Consulting Partners who scored above the median in EQ competencies, delivered $1.2 million more profit from their accounts than their other partners

→ An analysis of more than 300 top-level executives showed that six emotional competencies distinguished stars from the average: Influence, Team Leadership, Organisational Awareness, Self-confidence, Achievement Drive and Leadership

→ Insurance sales agents with high EQ sold over twice the amount of policies than their weaker counterparts.

Source: EI Consortium

Panel 1.5

High EQ can Improve...

→ Sales and profitability

→ Employee and customer engagement

→ Team motivation and confidence

→ Influencing and communication skills

→ Ability to handle pressure and stress

→ Judgment and decision-making

→ Optimism and resilience.

Source: EI Consortium

EQ has a significant impact on the quality of your relationships, decisions and your general enjoyment of life.

Why EQ and IQ Complement Each Other

It is important to understand that EQ is not the opposite of IQ. In fact, EQ complements IQ. IQ is often referred to as a 'threshold' competence. It might get you hired for a job but will not necessarily get you promoted. In other words, IQ is important but to go from 'good to great,' you need to complement your IQ with EQ. Star performers have both. The following table highlights how IQ and EQ complement each other:

Panel 1.6

EQ and IQ

IQ and EQ	IQ A 'threshold' competence	EQ Essential for going from 'good to great'
Skills	Linguistic	Self-awareness and management of emotions
	Analytical	Social skills
	Spatial orientation	Flexibility
	Logical reasoning	Self-motivation
		Optimism and resilience
Fixed or flexible?	Fixed by aged 17	Increases with life experience and development

Dispelling the Myths about EQ

→ **Myth 1 : 'EQ is about being 'nice' all the time!'** An effective leader has no problem disagreeing with his colleague if he holds a different point of view. However, when and how he deals with it is the key. Failing to confront or address issues is a sign of low EQ

→ **Myth 2 : 'Negative emotions are of no value to us'** On the contrary, negative emotions give us powerful signals that a change of behaviour or attitude is required

→ **Myth 3 :'You are born either emotionally intelligent or not'** EQ is to some extent linked with our personality and our life experience. It is a mixture of nurture and nature. Unlike IQ, however, EQ can be enhanced and developed.

EQ Can be Learned and Developed!

The good news is that EQ can be learned and developed. Our brains have a high level of 'plasticity' and can be rewired to change behaviours. EQ can be improved with increased self-awareness, coaching and support. We will be recommending strategies for EQ development throughout the book to help you on your journey!

Summary of Chapter 1

Let's jog your memory of this Chapter!

→ Emotional Intelligence, (EQ), is about being smart with your emotions. It is the ability to successfully manage yourself and your relationships with others. EQ is more commonly referred to as 'advanced commonsense'

→ People with high EQ are generally more self-confident, communicate better, manage stress effectively and have a positive outlook on life. This brings about increased success in both their personal and professional lives

→ The concept of 'Emotional Intelligence,' was originally developed by Mayer and Salovey and popularised by Daniel Goleman in his best-selling book 'Emotional Intelligence.' It was further developed for the leadership arena by Martyn Newman with the 'Emotional Capital Model™'

→ Increasing demands are being placed on today's leaders. This calls for an ability to successfully manage ourselves and engage our people, customers and other stakeholders

→ High EQ is associated with increased sales and profitability; improved employee and customer engagement; team motivation and confidence; effective influencing and communication skills; ability to handle pressure; better judgment and greater optimism and resilience

→ EQ is as important, if not more important than IQ in almost every role. While IQ matters, it is no longer enough in leadership roles. Highly effective leaders have a combination of both EQ and IQ

→ The No. 1 reason for career derailment is due to lack of EQ (Gallup)

→ Unlike IQ, EQ is not fixed and can be enhanced and developed through increased self-awareness, coaching and support.

The Power of Emotions

2

Chapter outline
The Power of Emotions

"When dealing with people, remember you are not dealing with creatures of logic but creatures of emotion."

Dale Carnegie

→ What are Emotions?
→ Why We Need to 'Tune in' to Them
→ The 'Emotional' and 'Thinking' Brain
→ Emotional 'Hijacking'
→ Rewiring the Brain to Develop New Behaviours!

Introduction

In this chapter, we define what emotions are and how they give us vital information for making good decisions, enhancing our relationships and maximising our personal effectiveness. We also take a look at the human brain and see that it has both an 'emotional' and 'thinking' dimension, both of which are inextricably linked.

Finally, we learn that the human brain has a high level of 'plasticity' and can, with practice and commitment, learn new behaviours. In other words, we can learn to become more emotionally intelligent!

What are Emotions?

> **Definition:**
>
> **Emotion (E*mo"tion), n.**
>
> *(L. Emovere - to shake, stir up; to move)*
>
> *Emotions are an inner source of* **energy, influence and information.** *They are contagious!*

Emotions are "primary motivating forces or processes which arouse, sustain and direct activity" (Leeper, 1948). They are physical sensations that drive us to act and are associated with energy. Motivation is ultimately related to emotion and people or events can inspire strong positive or negative emotions.

Feelings, the physical sensations that accompany our emotions, can be divided into one of three categories:

→ Physiological: hunger, nausea, tension, headaches

→ Emotional: anger, anxiety, happiness

→ Intuitive: 'gut' feelings and inner knowing

Source: Sparrow and Knight, (2006)

In her book, 'Molecules of Emotion,' neuroscientist Candace Pert explores the brain-body connection. Her research suggests that emotions do not occur just in the brain but appear to be based in biochemical reactions that occur throughout the body. Hence, one often hears *"I felt it in my gut,"* or *"I got cold feet."*

Why We Need to 'Tune in' to Them

Scientists believe that emotions are one of the fundamental traits associated with being human. Dan Siegal, author of 'Mindsight: The New Science of Personal Transformation,' states that effective interactions are based on the smooth integration of four key life skills: self-awareness, empathy, self-mastery and social skills. He argues that self-awareness is the foundation upon which these are based. If we are unable to tune in to our own emotions, we will find it more difficult to attune to those of others.

"Business is not just a numbers affair. I've never been particularly good at numbers but I'm convinced that it is feelings that account for the success of the Virgin brand in all of its myriad forms."

Richard Branson, CEO Virgin

16

Panel 2.1

The Power of Emotion©

E	Enables us to pick up valuable signals about self and others
M	Motivates us to take action
O	Occurs as whole body experience
T	Transforms our interactions with others
I	Indicates when we are overwhelmed or stressed
O	Optimises creativity and innovation
N	Navigates our decision-making process

It is important to highlight that emotions provide us with vital and potentially profitable information every minute of the day. Negative emotions can also be valuable as they give us a SIGNAL that a change is required.

Panel 2.2

Emotions give us Signals...

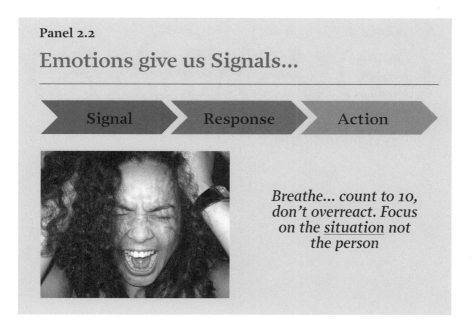

Signal ▶ Response ▶ Action

Breathe... count to 10, don't overreact. Focus on the <u>situation</u> not the person

→ Feeling **nervous** about an upcoming presentation to the senior management team? These feelings might signal that you need to **prepare** and **rehearse**

→ **Frustrated** with a colleague? This might suggest that you need to **pause** and **adapt** your communication style

→ An **angry** outburst? This might indicate that you are **overwhelmed** by too many demands and need to take time out.

Tuning in to Your Emotions

We are capable of experiencing hundreds of emotions but many of these emotions are variations of the six primary emotions: joy, surprise, disgust, fear, anger and sadness (Ekman, 1972).

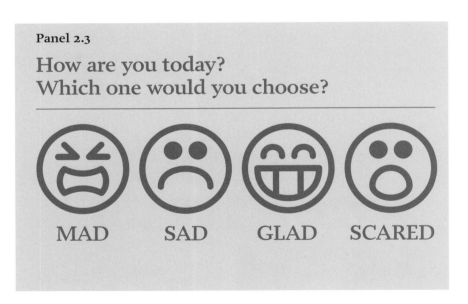

Panel 2.3

How are you today?
Which one would you choose?

MAD   SAD   GLAD   SCARED

How 'tuned in' are you?

Using the table below, think of a recent situation which made you feel happy or a situation which really made you angry or sad?

What was the level of intensity of your emotions at that time? How do you feel about that situation now on reflection? In what types of situation do you experience LOW or HIGH emotion?

Panel 2.4

Level of Intensity in our Emotions

Intensity	Happy	Sad	Angry	Scared
High	Elated	Depressed	Furious	Terrified
	Excited	Disappointed	Enraged	Horrified
	Overjoyed	Alone	Outraged	Scared Stiff
Medium	Cheerful	Heartbroken	Upset	Scared
	Up	Down	Mad	Frightened
	Good	Upset	Hot	Threatened
Low	Glad	Unhappy	Perturbed	Apprehensive
	Contented	Moody	Annoyed	Nervous
	Pleasant	Blue	Uptight	Worried

Source: Adapted from Bradbury and Greaves, (2003)

The 'Emotional' and 'Thinking' Brain

Advances in MRI technology and in neuroscience indicate that we have an 'emotional' brain as well as a 'thinking' brain, which are inextricably linked. Research has also revealed that we are primarily emotional decision-makers. Think about the last car you bought. What prompted your last purchase of designer face cream? Was your decision to purchase driven by logic or emotion? Studies show that emotions are twice as important as facts in making buying decisions (Morris *et al*, 2002).

To fully understand EQ, it is useful to examine the evolution of the human brain. In its basic form, our ancestors had only a root brain, (Reptilian), which controlled basic survival functions like breathing and metabolism. Fear of something would cause a 'fight or flight' response. We either confronted it head-on or ran away.

"...emotions are twice as important as facts in making buying decisions."

Morris *et al*, 2002

As we developed as a species, this brain evolved outwards forming what is known as the limbic or emotional centre of the brain. This unconscious part of the brain is where we store our values, attitudes and beliefs and also our emotional memories. Later, we developed the neocortex or 'thinking' brain, which gives humans the unique ability to stop and think about our behaviours before we blindly act upon them.

Panel 2.5

The Human Brain

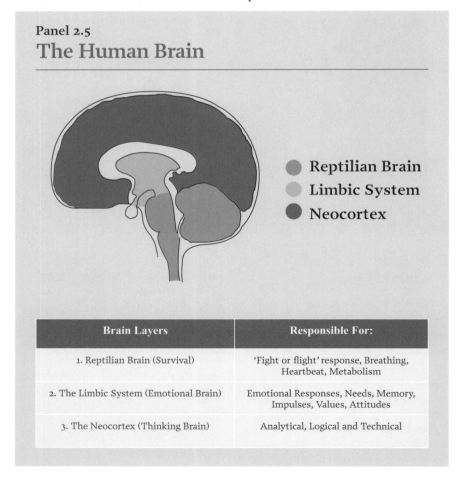

Reptilian Brain
Limbic System
Neocortex

Brain Layers	Responsible For:
1. Reptilian Brain (Survival)	'Fight or flight' response, Breathing, Heartbeat, Metabolism
2. The Limbic System (Emotional Brain)	Emotional Responses, Needs, Memory, Impulses, Values, Attitudes
3. The Neocortex (Thinking Brain)	Analytical, Logical and Technical

Panel 2.6

Remember... Emotions are Contagious!

Emotions are contagious like ripples in a pond

Our brains can react to the environment and change based on the people around us. This has the effect of putting us unconsciously on the same wavelength.
When a leader is very positive and approachable, people feel enthusiastic and function better. However, if the leader is critical or angry, it can affect everyone on the team and can negatively impact their performance.

According to Newman, *"Emotional intelligence requires effective communication between the rational and emotional centres of the brain. A broadband connection between these centres helps us make judgments and make choices and is critical for developing emotional intelligence."*

Panel 2.7

The extent to which the 'emotional' and 'thinking' brain communicate is at the core of emotional intelligence.

Emotional 'Hijacking'

At times, our emotions can hijack our 'thinking' brain and our sense of logic. I'm sure you can recall a situation when you said or did something suddenly that you later regretted. On reflection, it was probably irrational and completely 'out of character.'

Remember the 2006 World Cup Final? Why, in front of almost 30 billion viewers in 213 countries, did Zinedine Zidane, a highly successful role model, lose his self-control and head butt an opponent who had whispered a personal insult in his ear. There was certainly no logic for doing this, yet within seconds, a towering football career was brought abruptly to an end.

This emotional 'hijack' demonstrated to the world how easy it is to 'derail' in seconds if you can't control your emotions. This is also referred to as an "amygdala hijack," a term first coined by Daniel Goleman. This is the part of the brain that regulates the 'fight or flight' response. When threatened, we can respond irrationally. A rush of stress hormones flood the body before the neocortex can rationalise what is happening. Circumstances could have been so different, had Zidane been more self-aware and in control of his emotions.

> "The essential difference between emotion and reason, is that emotion leads to action while reason leads to conclusions."
>
> Dr. Donald B. Calne, Professor of Neurology, University of British Columbia

Therefore, take time to consciously tune in to both your emotions and your thinking as this can lead to positive action! Emotions can provide us with a powerful resource to guide our decision-making.

"Anyone can become angry - that is easy, but to be angry with the right person at the right time, and for the right reason and in the right way... that is not easy."

Aristotle

Rewiring Our Brain to Develop New Behaviours!

One of the most interesting recent findings in the field of neuroscience, is that the brain has a high level of 'plasticity,' or the ability to change. While people seem to be born with particular temperaments already in place, repeated **positive behaviours and experiences can actually alter the structure of the brain**, rewiring it to establish new behaviours (Siegal, 2007). Siegal argues that when we become more aware of our thoughts and feelings, we can then proactively 'rewire' the brain to develop new behaviours.

For example, if we recall the TACT© approach in Chapter One, we can choose to consciously *tune in* to how we are feeling and what emotion we are experiencing when we are angry, or when something does not go 'our way.' Do you feel hurt because the individual whom you relied upon has let you down? Or are you frustrated and annoyed because the other person's actions have resulted in you being late again for an important meeting?

By paying attention to our emotions and the signals they are giving us, we can consciously adapt our behaviour.

"...positive behaviours and experiences can actually alter the structure of the brain, rewiring it to establish new behaviours."

Dan Siegal

Summary of Chapter 2

Let's jog your memory of this Chapter!

→ "When dealing with people, remember that you are not dealing with creatures of logic, but creatures of emotion" Dale Carnegie

→ Emotions are a powerful source of energy, influence and information. Emotions have many benefits if we pay attention to them:

- They can give us valuable signals about ourselves, other people and situations

- Emotions, negative and positive, can be experienced throughout the body and are contagious

- They are essential for good judgment and effective decision-making

- Positive emotions can generate enthusiasm, creativity and optimism within an organisation

- Negative emotions give us vital signals for adapting our behaviour. Ignoring them can sabotage our relationships and our business

- While our thoughts lead to conclusions, emotions propel us to action

→ We have both a 'thinking' and 'feeling' brain which are inextricably linked. The extent to which the 'emotional' and 'thinking' brains communicate is at the core of emotional intelligence

→ An emotional 'hijack' can work against us causing career derailment and a breakdown in relationships

→ Our brains have a high level of 'plasticity' and can be rewired to learn new behaviours.

Why is EQ so Critical for Today's Leader?

3

Chapter outline
Why is EQ so Critical for Today's Leader?

"The quality of leadership, more than any other single factor, determines the success or failure of an organisation."

Fiedler and Chemers, (2002)

→ Challenges Facing Today's Leader
→ A New Style of Leadership Beckons
→ Adapting Your Leadership Style: "Choosing the Right Club for Each Shot!"
→ Why EQ is Now an 'Imperative' for Effective Leadership
→ Emotional Capitalists - Creating Competitive Advantage

Introduction

In this chapter, we explore why today's challenging environment calls for a new style of leadership and why EQ is at the heart of this leadership.

We then define the business case for EQ and its importance as a competitive advantage. Finally we outline the 10 critical EQ competencies for personal and interpersonal effectiveness.

Challenges Facing Today's Leader

In today's challenging marketplace, leaders face constant change. As highlighted in chapter one, businesses are under pressure to constantly innovate while at the same time, keep a close eye on operational costs and achieve more with less. Global competition, the rise and rise of the BRIC economies, (Brazil, Russia, India and China), increasing consumer demands, faster product cycles and the advance of new technologies have dramatically changed the way we do business. As Ray Stata, co-founder and chairman of Analog Devices once said, *"the rate at which individuals and organisations learn may become the only sustainable competitive advantage."* Therefore, the primary responsibility of any leader is to create an environment which can attract, retain, develop and grow the best and brightest employees.

As a result of the accelerated growth of the knowledge economy, the psychological contract between employer and employee has changed. Rene Carayol, Leadership expert, tells us, *"position and job title no longer make you a leader - you need to 'earn' your leadership."* Today IQ and technical competence are no longer enough to successfully lead a team. The old leadership style of 'command and control,' that was once typical in business, now needs to be replaced by a much more collaborative approach.

Great leaders can articulate and engage people with a compelling vision and values and have a determination to succeed, even in tough times. Ronald Heifetz, in his book, 'Leadership with No Easy Answers,' argues that "the real heroism of leadership involves having the courage to face reality and mobilising others to tackle tough challenges" (Heifetz, 2004).

> "The real heroism of leadership involves having the courage to face reality and mobilising others to tackle tough challenges."
>
> Heifetz, 2004

The leader therefore, can no longer rely solely on their IQ or technical competence to lead successfully. As Daniel Pink tells us, there is now a clear shift from 'left brain,' logical and analytical abilities, to an increasing focus on 'right brain' skills such as inventiveness, empathy and instilling meaning and purpose among employees (Daniel Pink, author of 'A Whole New Mind'). This transition from the 'old' to a 'new' collaborative style of leadership is shown on the next page:

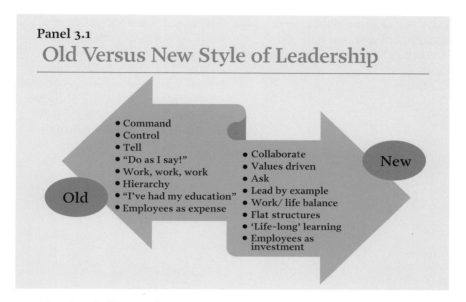

Panel 3.1

Old Versus New Style of Leadership

Old
- Command
- Control
- Tell
- "Do as I say!"
- Work, work, work
- Hierarchy
- "I've had my education"
- Employees as expense

New
- Collaborate
- Values driven
- Ask
- Lead by example
- Work/ life balance
- Flat structures
- 'Life-long' learning
- Employees as investment

Despite the challenges facing him, the level of charisma and EQ demonstrated by President Barack Obama is clearly evident. When we examine his inauguration speech, only the first seven minutes related to his campaign. In the remainder of his address, he was able to tap into the emotional needs of the American people and urge them to support change, *"Yes, we can!"* Obama clearly demonstrated the leader's role to provide clarity and hope in times of adversity. EQ is the ability to inspire and tap into people's values so that they want to move towards the new vision *with* you.

Other great charismatic leaders, such as Martin Luther King Jnr., Mahatma Ghandi and Nelson Mandela have inspired followers though their quiet humility and conviction. They led by example, with dignity, courage and determination.

A New Style of Leadership Beckons

To be successful in today's challenging environment, leaders must adopt a much more resilient and proactive approach and be able to interact effectively with others.

EQ is now a key factor that "differentiates great leaders from average leaders"

Goleman, 2005

When the Gallup organisation examined employee engagement worldwide in 2005, they discovered that only 29% of employees were fully engaged and committed to the organisation, 54% were just present, and alarmingly, 17% were completely disengaged.

With such a clear link between engagement and productivity, it is critical that leaders inspire, motivate and engage employees for the future.

Goffee and Jones (2006) pointedly ask, "Why should anyone be led by you?" and wait for knees to shake! They firmly believe that leaders cannot operate without the commitment and loyalty of their followers. In their studies, they identified **four key elements** that followers want from leaders:

Panel 3.2

What Employees Want

Source: Adapted from Goffee and Jones (2006), 'Why Should Anyone be Led by You?'

→ **Authenticity:** there's no point trying to emulate someone else - lead authentically and be yourself

→ **Significance:** provide meaning and significance in the work people do

→ **Excitement:** inspire passion and enthusiasm to follow a shared vision

→ **Community:** create an atmosphere of camaraderie and trust

"Leadership must always be viewed as a relationship between the leader and the led."

Goffee and Jones, 2006

EQ in leadership is also about awareness and responsibility. Leaders need to be aware of their own personal leadership style and the impact their behaviour has on others. At the same time, they must be able to adapt their behaviour depending on the context of the situation they are faced with and in their relationships with others. This is highlighted in the model below:

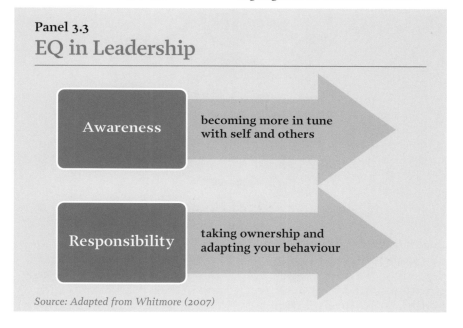

Panel 3.3

EQ in Leadership

Awareness — becoming more in tune with self and others

Responsibility — taking ownership and adapting your behaviour

Source: Adapted from Whitmore (2007)

Everyone can recall the horror of 9/11, when New Yorkers were devastated by the terrorist attack on the World Trade Centre. One leader, who emerged in this crisis and stepped up to the challenge, was New York Mayor, Rudi Giuliani. He seemed to capture the mood of the nation when he summed up the feeling of despair. When asked how many people had suffered he answered, "We do not know how many but what we do know is that it will be more than we can bear."

EQ is at the heart of successful leadership. In their research, Kouzes and Posner, authors of 'The Leadership Challenge,' identified five key practices that great leaders demonstrate in *"achieving extraordinary things through ordinary people."*

These practices require strong EQ in order to gain the commitment and engagement of followers:

Panel 3.4

The Five Practices of Great Leadership

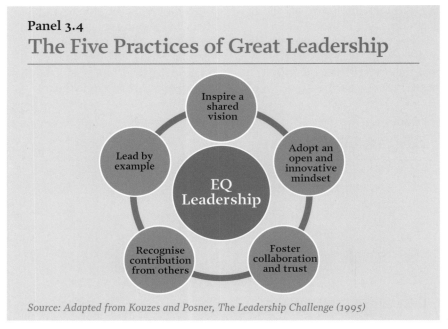

Source: Adapted from Kouzes and Posner, The Leadership Challenge (1995)

Emotionally-intelligent leaders are also aware that every interaction depends on the **context or situation** at hand. Therefore, great leaders are able to **adapt** their leadership style appropriately.

Adapting Your Leadership Style: "Choosing the Right Club for Each Shot!"

There is no one best way to lead. Some successful leaders are more reserved and humble, such as CEO P. J. Lafley in Proctor & Gamble or CEO Cork Walgreen of Walgreen PLC, head of one of the highly successful companies cited by Jim Collins in 'Good to Great.' Others, such as Jack Welch, former CEO of General Electric, are strong charismatics who go with their 'gut' instincts.

Skilful leaders authentically work to their strengths and adapt appropriately in a given situation and in their relationships with others. They must be able to adapt to any given context like *"authentic chameleons"* (Goffee and Jones, 2006).

Different people and situations call for different styles of leadership. For example, in the midst of a merger or acquisition, a diplomatic negotiator is required, whereas in a turnaround situation, the leader's role is to encourage and motivate people to follow a new direction.

Goleman compares these leadership styles to golf clubs in a seasoned professional's bag, and emphasises the importance of *"choosing the right club for each shot."*

"Choosing the right club for each shot!"

Source: Goleman, 2005

He outlines a number of different leadership styles which are used depending on the situation and circumstances the leader faces. Where change and a new direction is needed in an organisation, the authoritative style is most effective where people trust the leader in taking them towards a better future, despite the hardships. Leaders who have mastered four or more styles, especially the authoritative, affiliative, democratic and coaching styles and who can move seamlessly from one to the other depending on the situation, produce the most positive impact on organisational cultures and enjoy the greatest business success (Goleman, 2005).

Panel 3.5

The Adaptive Leader

Authoritative	Mobilises people towards a clear vision
Coaching	Develops people for the future
Affiliative	Creates harmony and builds emotional bonds
Democratic	Builds consensus through participation

Source: Adapted from Goleman, 2005

Why EQ is Now an 'Imperative' for Effective Leadership

As we have outlined above, the traditional key leadership skills such as strategic and analytical thinking and reasoning are still fundamental but they are no longer enough. People skills or 'soft' skills have now become the 'hard' skills in the business world. EQ is now a pre-requisite for current and future leaders.

From our review of the various EQ models, we outline the 10 key personal and interpersonal competencies that are an **IMPERATIVE** for effective leadership. These competencies are based on Martyn Newman's highly-validated and researched **Emotional Capital Model**™, which is specifically geared for the leadership arena.

Typical behaviours of the emotionally intelligent leader are highlighted in panel 3.6:

33

Panel 3.6
A Successful Leader...

I	Is in tune with own emotions and those of others
M	Manages these emotions productively
P	Projects a positive and resilient approach
E	Empathises and can read people well
R	Relates and communicates effectively
A	Adopts a flexible and open mindset
T	Tackles stress and pressure well
I	Is independent and assertive
V	Visualises and maximises his/her potential
E	Enjoys a high level of self-confidence

It is important to highlight that *balance* is key. Being 'strong' in a certain competence is not always effective unless it is in balance with other competencies, e.g. if a leader demonstrates a high level of 'assertiveness' yet lacks 'empathy,' he/she may not get the best out of his/her relationships both inside and outside the organisation.

Emotional Capitalists - Creating Competitive Advantage

"Emotional capitalists represent leaders with the advanced capacity of being able to guide people to action from within by engaging the prime movers of behaviour - emotions."

Dr. Martyn Newman

So what do these emotionally-intelligent leaders bring to the table? As Martyn Newman emphasises in his book *'Emotional*

Capitalists - The New Leaders,' to be really effective today, we need to work with a *"new balance sheet."* This is one that goes beyond the traditional assets such as the financial, physical and intellectual - to a new focus on 'emotional capital' and the things that engage and motivate your people, customers and stakeholders.

Newman refers to the leaders who display these emotional and social competencies as 'Emotional Capitalists.' They *"create value and influence through their capacity to*

identify with the emotional experience and aspirations of their people, and build shared identities with them."

Newman was the first to design a scientifically-valid psychometric tool that measures the specific EQ competencies linked to effective leadership performance. This tool, known as the ECR™, is based on the Emotional Capital Model™ of Emotional Intelligence, as shown below:

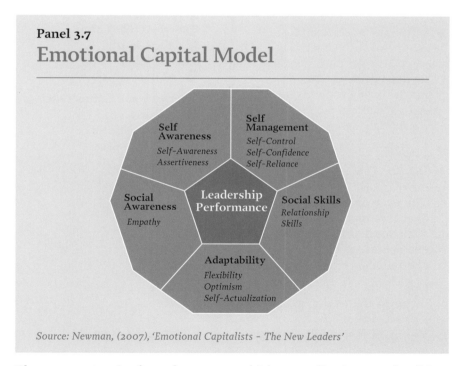

Panel 3.7
Emotional Capital Model

Self Awareness
Self-Awareness
Assertiveness

Self Management
Self-Control
Self-Confidence
Self-Reliance

Social Awareness
Empathy

Leadership Performance

Social Skills
Relationship Skills

Adaptability
Flexibility
Optimism
Self-Actualization

Source: Newman, (2007), 'Emotional Capitalists - The New Leaders'

These competencies form the two pillars of EQ success: Personal and Interpersonal Effectiveness, which we outline in more detail in Chapters four and five.

Summary of Chapter 3

Let's jog your memory of this Chapter!

→ Today's leaders are operating in an environment where change is the only constant and the need to achieve more with less is the norm

→ This changing environment calls for a shift from a 'command and control' approach to a more collaborative, inspirational, values-driven leadership approach, which underpins EQ

→ While the traditional IQ analytical and technical stills are still important, they are no longer enough. EQ is increasingly becoming a more critical success factor for today's leader

→ A combination of both IQ and EQ skills create a more 'rounded' leader

→ There are four principle elements that employees want: authenticity, meaning, excitement and a feeling of community

→ Great leaders lead by example, inspire a shared vision, adopt an open and innovative approach, foster collaboration and trust and recognise and honour the contribution of others

→ There is no one best way to lead. An effective leader needs to be able to *"choose the right club for each shot,"* depending on the context

→ Martyn Newman's Emotional Capital Model™ captures 10 key competencies for effective leadership. These competencies form the two pillars of EQ success which we outline in Chapters four and five:

- **Personal Competencies:**
  ① Self-Awareness,
  ② Self-Confidence,
  ③ Self-Reliance,
  ④ Self-Actualisation,
  ⑤ Self-Control,
  ⑥ Flexibility,
  ⑦ Optimism/Resilience

- **Interpersonal Competencies:**
  ⑧ Empathy,
  ⑨ Relationship skills,
  ⑩ Assertiveness

→ The key message is to have a **balanced approach.**

Notes

Section II
The Two Pillars of EQ Success - Personal & Interpersonal Effectiveness

In this section, we explore further the 10 EQ competencies which differentiate outstanding leaders from the average and form the two pillars of EQ Success: personal and interpersonal effectiveness.

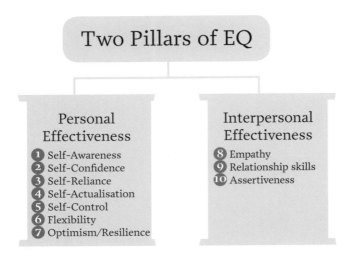

Two Pillars of EQ

Personal Effectiveness
1. Self-Awareness
2. Self-Confidence
3. Self-Reliance
4. Self-Actualisation
5. Self-Control
6. Flexibility
7. Optimism/Resilience

Interpersonal Effectiveness
8. Empathy
9. Relationship skills
10. Assertiveness

Personal Effectiveness - Knowing and Managing Self

4

Chapter outline
Personal Effectiveness: Knowing and Managing Self

"He who knows the universe and does not know himself, knows nothing."

Jean de la Fontaine

→ ❶ **Self-Awareness:** 'Tuning into your thoughts, feelings and motivations'

→ ❷ **Self-Confidence:** 'Being self-assured and comfortable in your own skin'

→ ❸ **Self-Reliance:** 'The buck stops with you!'

→ ❹ **Self-Actualisation:** 'Being self-motivated to achieve your full potential'

→ ❺ **Self-Control:** 'Staying calm and controlled under pressure'

→ ❻ **Flexibility:** 'Being open and responsive to change'

→ ❼ **Optimism and Resilience:** 'Adopting a positive mindset even in the face of setbacks'

Introduction

Great leadership starts with self. To be an effective leader, we must first know, understand and manage ourselves before we can influence others. In this chapter, we outline the personal EQ competencies which are essential for effective leadership and provide practical tips for developing each of them.

Highly effective leaders are aware of the need to maintain a sense of balance across all the competencies.

❶ Self-Awareness: 'tuning in to your thoughts, feelings and motivations'

> *"He who knows the universe but does not know himself, knows nothing"*
>
> Jean de la Fontaine

How good are you at tuning in to your thoughts and feelings at any particular time? How well do you understand what is driving your behaviour and the impact that this might have on other people? Are you aware of your unique strengths and weaknesses and what makes you tick?

Panel 4.1

Self-awareness is the **cornerstone** of all emotional intelligence and is recognised as the No.1 capability for effective leadership (Harvard Business Review, 2007). Obviously what you cannot recognise, you cannot manage!

Self-awareness allows us to stand back and examine the way we see ourselves. Emotionally-intelligent leaders are able to tune in and become the 'observer' of their thoughts, feelings and behaviours at any time. They can then interpret this valuable information and then choose an appropriate response. Self-awareness affects not only our attitudes and behaviours but also how we see other people.

Dan Siegal, author of 'Mindsights,' uses a very powerful metaphor, *"dive into the sea inside."* So often, we can become overwhelmed by different emotions. Therefore, by focusing our attention on these emotions, we can manage them instead of being 'swept away' with them (Siegal, 2010).

As you reflect on both Chapters 4 and 5, it is useful to recall the TACT© approach from Chapter One. It will provide you with four easy steps to develop your EQ. The TACT© approach will help you improve both your Personal and Interpersonal Effectiveness. This model reminds us to consciously 'tune in' to how we are feeling at any time; understand what emotion we are experiencing and that we have the ability to choose a more appropriate response before taking action.

Scenario

John's day starts badly. His car has broken down and he has forgotten his 'Blackberry,' which he left on the hall table at home. By the time he reaches the office, he is completely frustrated and uptight. He continues to be moody with everyone all day at work. However, if he had tuned in to that mood, understood the impact of his behaviour on others, he could have adapted his behaviour. As a result, the team around him would not have had to suffer the consequences and he would have had a much better day!

Panel 4.1

 **Self-Awareness:**

Self-Awareness	
High	**Low**
• can tune in to their thoughts and feelings at any time • are aware of how their behaviours impact others • are clear on their values and beliefs, i.e. what they stand for • know their strengths and 'ouch points'	• unaware of how their feelings and behaviours can impact both their performance and their interaction with others • poor awareness of their strengths and weaknesses

Where would you rate yourself on this scale?

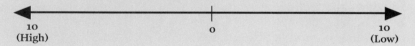

10
(High)

0

10
(Low)

Panel 4.2

How good are you at 'tuning in?'

Become an 'observer' of your thoughts and feelings. 'Tune in' to them and choose how to better manage yourself and your interactions with others.

Star Performer
Barack Obama

No matter what issue he is faced with, President Barack Obama is always aware of his image and how he presents himself for maximum impact. Grounded and reflective, he clearly demonstrates self-confidence and emotional self-awareness. He is well aware of his strengths and weaknesses in political office and has tapped into the strengths of former adversaries such as Hilary Clinton, to support his political aims.

◎ Practical Tips:

How did you rate yourself on the self-awareness scale? Here are some useful tips which you can work on to develop your self-awareness:

→ **Become the 'observer' of your thoughts and feelings**
By standing back and consciously observing yourself, you can pick up valuable signals which can help you better manage your own behaviour and your interaction with others

→ **Keep a journal**
Keep a journal to enhance self-awareness. Reflect on the highlights of the day. Ask yourself, how did you respond to the various situations? What did you learn? What would you do differently the next time?

→ **Pay attention to what your body is telling you**
Don't forget to pay attention to the physical signals your body is sending you, e.g. if you have a knot in your stomach, your body may be telling you to relax and take a break

→ **Practise mindfulness**
As Eckhart Tolle says in his book 'The Power of Now,' *"wherever you are, be there totally."* For example, when you are at a meeting, *be* **fully present** at the meeting instead of thinking about what you are going to do next

→ **Look for feedback from others and consider taking an EQ assessment**
Look for feedback from colleagues, mentors and friends and consider taking an EQ assessment with a professional coach to help you maximise your EQ strengths and focus on development areas.

❷ Self-Confidence:
'being self-assured and comfortable in your own skin'

"Our deepest fear is not that we are inadequate. Our deepest fear is that we are powerful beyond measure."

Marianne Williamson

How good do you feel about yourself? Are you confident in your skills and abilities? Do you usually feel you are going to succeed at something you set your mind to? Are you able to acknowledge your mistakes and move on?

Leaders with a high level of self-confidence are self-assured and are very 'comfortable in their own skin'. They generally accept and feel good about themselves, 'warts and all.' They can recognise and leverage their unique strengths as well as being able to acknowledge their limitations and mistakes.

Panel 4.3

② Self-Confidence:

Self-Confidence	
High	**Low**
• have high self-belief about what they can achieve	• have little confidence in their abilities
• are comfortable in their own skin	• sometimes compensate by exaggerating their competences publicly
• recognise their strengths and limitations	
• acknowledge their mistakes and move on	• take things personally and are very defensive
• don't take things personally	• can find it difficult to express their viewpoints

Where would you rate yourself on this scale?

←————————————————|————————————————→

10
(High)

0

10
(Low)

Three little words

"I was wrong."

Sometimes they can be the hardest words to say but once articulated, leaders tend to gain more respect and trust from their team, customers and colleagues.

When American Air Force One flew over the skies of New York on a PR exercise, officials were completely unaware of the terror it would create in the eyes and ears of New Yorkers after the trauma of 9/11. President

Barack Obama immediately came 'on air' and said he "messed up." He was not afraid to take responsibility for a major error of judgment even though he knew nothing about the incident or had not approved it.

Star Performer
Muhammed Ali ★

Muhammed Ali set himself very high goals and had an absolute belief about achieving them. No challenge was insurmountable.

Even in his retirement, his confidence has matured and despite his illness, he persists in helping to make the world a better place.

"I know where I'm going and I know the truth and I don't have to be what you want me to be. I'm free to be what I want."

Muhammed Ali

◎ Practical Tips:

How did you rate yourself on the self-confidence scale? Here are some useful tips which you can work on to develop your self-confidence:

→ **The Trophy Room**

- Reflect on your past achievements and successes

- Document and update these positive highlights in writing on a regular basis

- Keep and reflect on mementoes, positive reports from colleagues, prizes, photos and inspirational quotes

- Compile your favourite inspirational music to give you positive energy when you need it!

→ **'Walk the Walk, Look the Part!'**
Remember that your physical posture and appearance reveal a lot about you. *"Be"* confident! 'Fake it till you make it!' Hold your shoulders back and smile! Also, remember that how you dress can project a professional or unprofessional image of yourself!

→ **Pay attention to your self-talk!**
According to psychologists, we have approximately 50,000 thoughts per day. Make sure you filter out the negative ones and replace them with more positive ones!

→ **Visualisation**
To build confidence before a difficult meeting or an upcoming presentation, visualise the desired outcome beforehand as though it has gone really well. In sport, many successful athletes visualise winning the race before they have even left the starting blocks - they see themselves crossing the finish line, hearing the applause and feeling the intense feeling of pride and satisfaction

→ **Don't take things personally**
Remember, you have the power to choose how to respond to situations. As Eleanor Roosevelt said, *"No-one can make you feel inferior without your consent"*

→ **Just be yourself!**
Don't try to be like anyone else. Leverage your strengths and uniqueness to be your authentic self.

❸ Self-Reliance "the buck stops with you!"

> *"The very definition of being a leader means you are out in front - with no-one else. Taking the road less travelled."*
>
> Robin Sharma,
> 'The Greatness Guide'

To what extent do you take responsibility for yourself and your leadership role? Or do you depend too much on others when making decisions? How comfortable are you about taking unpopular decisions when called for?

Self-reliance is about having independence of thought and taking responsibility for your actions and the consequences.

Successful leaders, while collaborating with their team, are courageous in making tough calls when they have to.

Self-reliance also relates to the individual's 'locus of control.' Those with a high external locus of control, believe that powerful others, fate, or chance primarily determine events. People with a high internal locus of control, on the other hand, tend to believe that events result primarily from their own behaviour and that they have the power to influence their environment. However, it is important for them to be aware of the impact this may be having on others. We could be highly self-reliant and single-minded, without realising that we are unconsciously 'shutting other people out.' If you would like to measure your 'locus of control' you can find a useful questionnaire in the Chapter 7.

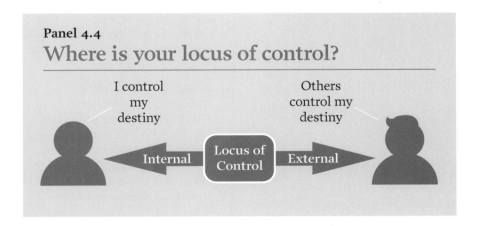

Panel 4.4
Where is your locus of control?

I control my destiny

Others control my destiny

Internal — Locus of Control — External

Panel 4.5

③ Self-Reliance:

Self-Reliance	
High	**Low**
• take full responsibility for their actions and consequences	• can be slow to make decisions on their own
• enjoy taking control and leading others	• tend to be overly dependent on others to lead them
• while collaborating with their team, are confident in their own judgment	• tend to look for ongoing support and approval from others
• can make tough, unpopular decisions where necessary	

Where would you rate yourself on this scale?

```
◄─────────────────┼─────────────────►
10                 0                 10
(High)                              (Low)
```

Star Performer

Rosa Parks

"I have learned over the years that when one's mind is made up, this diminishes fear; knowing what must be done does away with fear."

Rosa Parks

Parks' refusal to give up her seat on the bus home was instrumental in stimulating the civil rights movement across America.

 Practical Tips:

How did you rate yourself on the self-reliance scale? Here are some useful tips which you can work on to develop your self-reliance:

→ **Take responsibility!**
Accept personal responsibility for your own thoughts, feelings and action. Remember that 'the buck stops with you!'

→ **Recall past successful independent behaviour**
Call to mind situations when you have taken a decision independently and it has gone well. How did you feel? You know that you have done it before, so there's no reason you cannot do it again! Keep building on these successes

48

→ **Keep a journal**
Record and review instances during the day when you have acted or not acted independently:

- What made you do what you did?

- How did it feel?

- What have you learned?

"The greatest danger for most of us lies not in setting our aim too high and falling short, but in setting it too low and achieving our mark."

Michelangelo

❹ Self-Actualisation: 'being self-motivated to achieve your full potential'

Are you maximising your talents to their full potential? What really inspires you? Are you passionate and motivated about being the best that you can be? Are you engaged in activities and interests that really matter to you in both your professional and personal life?

In order to ignite passion in others, a leader must be passionate themselves. Emotionally-intelligent leaders tend to live life to the full and have a clear sense of purpose which is consistent with their values.

Panel 4.6

❹ Self-Actualisation:

Self Actualisation	
High	Low
• are highly motivated to reach their full potential	• are unclear about their personal direction
• are engaged and passionate about things that really matter to them	• tend to be unfulfilled in their job
• enjoy setting challenging personal and professional goals	• are not maximising their talents and strengths
• live a life that is consistent with their values	• have a poor work/life balance

Where would you rate yourself on this scale?

```
◄───────────────────┼───────────────────►
10                    0                    10
(High)                                   (Low)
```

Star Performer

Richard Branson

At school, Sir Richard Branson struggled with dyslexia and was never very good with figures, yet he is now known as one of the world's most successful businessmen. When asked what motivates him, he said:

"My interest in life comes from setting myself huge, apparently unachievable challenges and trying to rise above them...from the perspective of wanting to live life to the full."

Richard Branson,
Entrepreneur

Panel 4.7

Purpose and Passion:

"Successful leaders and entrepreneurs have a passionate belief in what they are doing, a passion that sustains them through the tough times."

Charles Handy,
The New Alchemists

◎ Practical Tips:

How did you rate yourself on the self-actualisation scale? Here are some useful tips which you can work on to develop your self-actualisation:

→ **What fuels your passion?**

- Who or what inspires you? What are you passionate about?

- What are your unique talents and gifts?

- Who do you want to be? What do you want to learn?

→ **What do you stand for?**
What is important to you in your life? What are your values? Are you living a life consistent with these values? For more details, complete the 'Values Audit' in Chapter 7

→ **What do you want to be remembered for?**
What legacy do you want to leave behind? What would you like

50

your spouse or partner, friends, family and colleagues to say about you?

→ **What's your big audacious dream?**
What would ignite a 'fire in your belly' and make you get out of your comfort zone? Bill Gates from Microsoft wanted to put a computer in every household. President J. F. Kennedy's vision was to put a man on the moon. What is YOURS?

→ **Strive for a healthy work/life balance**
Are you all work and no play? Do you engage in your hobbies as much as you would like to? How good are you at staying in touch with family and friends? See Chapter 7 for further exercises to help you build greater work-life balance.

❺ Self-Control: 'staying calm and controlled under pressure'

> *"The most valuable time we have is between stimulus and response."*
>
> Stephen R. Covey

How good are you at staying composed and resisting an impulse? How well do you cope with pressure and stressful situations? Do you tend to rush into decisions which you may later regret?

Self-control is about how you manage your response under pressure. It is the ability to resist or delay an impulse. Leaders with high self-control remain calm in stressful and pressurised situations and make considered decisions in a composed manner.

Panel 4.8
❺ Self-Control:

Self-Control	
High	**Low**
• stay calm and composed under pressure	• tend to be impulsive and predictable
• rarely 'lose the head'	• can be 'hot headed' and prone to anger
• not impulsive	• can get overwhelmed and stressed easily
• can withstand high stress levels	

Where would you rate yourself on this scale?

⬅————————————|————————————➡
10
(High)   0   10
(Low)

Managing Stress

> *"We cannot direct the wind but we can adjust the sails."*
>
> Dolly Parton

Normal levels of stress or *'eustress'* can be a positive influence in our everyday life in helping us perform at our optimum peak. However, *'distress'* or negative stress, occurs when there is an imbalance between our perceived demands versus the perceived resources available to meet those demands. Studies show that 75-90% of all visits to front-line health professionals are due to stress-related disorders (Rosch, HeartMath.com).

Each individual has a different capacity to withstand stress and the key is to recognise the triggers of what stresses you and how you proactively cope with that trigger or situation.

Panel 4.9

Stress: Balancing Demands and Resources

Star Performer

Roger Federer

Roger Federer, grand slam record holder, appears to epitomise a calm demeanour on the court at all times, despite the tremendous pressure he is under. Was he always that way? Did you know that Bjorn Borg, winner of 11 grand slams did not always have an ice cool temperament on court? In his early days, he was suspended from his club for six months for throwing rackets. When he came back, he channelled all that anger into concentration and staying focused. In other words he managed to use the negative energy from his frustration in a positive way.

◎ Practical Tips:

How did you rate yourself on the self-control scale? Here are some

useful tips which you can work on to develop your self-control:

→ **Name, Claim, Reframe and Aim!**

Panel 4.10

Name Claim Reframe Aim!

Name	Identify what you are feeling, e.g "I'm furious," "That's the last straw!" (Anger)
Claim	Acknowledge and accept you are feeling this way: "I feel really angry with Joe for losing the file."
Reframe	Reframe the situation in a more positive light: Count to 10. "It will turn up. We're all under pressure. I'll take the best action I can in the circumstances."
Aim!	Proactively decide to do something constructive about it: "It's not so bad. I have back up copies on the computer which I can download. Let's do it now!"

→ **Know your 'hot buttons'**
'Tune in' to what triggers stress for you

→ **Only focus your energy on things you <u>can</u> control**
There are certain things that we can control and those which are outside our control. Focus your energy only on things you can do something about

→ **Plan, prioritise and learn to say 'NO'**
Set goals and priorities for your work. Stick to your plan as much as possible to prevent overloading at the last minute. Don't forget to incorporate time for mini-breaks of 10-15 minutes. Every time you say 'yes' to something trivial, you say 'no' to something important! Saying 'no' is saying 'yes' to yourself

→ **Pause...Smile!...Breathe**
Pause, count to 10. Pausing gives us time to consider an appropriate response. Relax your shoulders and breathe a little deeper

→ **Uplift your mood by playing your favourite music!**
Listening to your favourite music can really lift your spirits. Put together some playlists of your favourite tracks for different situations: e.g. 'relaxation'; 'boost energy'; 'power walking'

→ **Take some exercise!**
Research shows that by taking regular exercise we release 'endorphins' or happy hormones which make us feel better and give us more energy

→ **Talk things out with a trusted colleague or friend**
A problem shared is a problem halved. Often by talking through things with someone else when you are under pressure can give you a more positive perspective.

❻ Flexibility: 'being open and responsive to change'

"It is not the strongest of the species that survives nor the most intelligent...it is the one that is the most adaptable to change."

Charles Darwin

How open are you to change? How willing are you to change your mind, when the evidence suggests that you are mistaken? How easily do you adapt to unfamiliar experiences, events and ideas? How good are you at taking an innovative approach on things?

Emotionally-intelligent leaders are able to adjust their emotions and behaviours to changing situations and new ideas. The ability to embrace unpredictable circumstances is a key hallmark of success.

Panel 4.11

❻ Flexibility:

Flexibility	
High	**Low**
• are open and adaptable to unfamiliar and changing situations	• can be set in their ways; play it safe
• can handle multiple demands with ease	• adopt the motto: "if it ain't broke, don't fix it"
• willing to change their minds if the evidence suggests that they are mistaken	• want to be 'right' at all costs
• take fresh approaches and risks in their thinking	• can be rigid and slow to change

Where would you rate yourself on this scale?

←————————————|————————————→

10
(High)   0   10
(Low)

Remember...flexibility must be applied in context
One should never be flexible to the point of compromising one's values and desired outcomes.

"In this dynamic global environment only adaptive individuals and organisations will thrive."

Kouzes and Posner, (2005)

◎ Practical Tips:

How did you rate yourself on the flexibility scale? Here are some useful tips which you can work on to develop your flexibility:

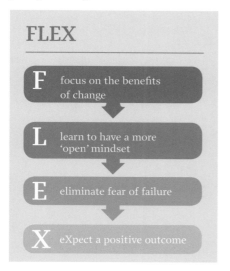

FLEX

F focus on the benefits of change

L learn to have a more 'open' mindset

E eliminate fear of failure

X eXpect a positive outcome

→ **Focus on the benefits of change**
When faced with new circumstances and imminent change, write down a list of reasons why this change might bring new benefits and opportunities

→ **Learn to have a more 'open' mindset**
Encourage group brainstorming to get different viewpoints before you rush into making decisions. This will help you see the big picture and put things into perspective

→ **Eliminate fear of failure**
Reduce the fear factor by talking things out with others. Recall past experiences when change worked out well. Also, as the author Susan Jeffers says, sometimes you have to *"FEEL THE FEAR and do it anyway!"*

→ **eXpect a positive yet realistic outcome**
Remember that, if you expect things to work out positively, they are more likely to turn out that way.

❼ Optimism and Resilience: 'adopting a positive mindset even in the face of setbacks'

"The ultimate measure of a man is not where he stands in moments of comfort and convenience, but where he stands at times of challenge and controversy."

Dr. Martin Luther King Jr

Are you a person who sees the glass half full or half empty? How do you experience setbacks - do you see them as problems or challenges? Are you generally motivated to continue, even when the going gets really tough?

Leaders with high optimism and resilience see the 'glass half full' and maintain a positive attitude even in tough times. They recognise when they are in a difficult situation but adopt a 'can do' approach in dealing with it. They tend to be more resilient and look at setbacks as learning opportunities for personal growth. While they have that quality of 'bouncebackability,' they maintain a strong sense of realism.

Who am I?

Failed in business at age 21

Was defeated in a legislative race at age 22

Failed again in business at age 24

Overcame the death of his girlfriend at age 26

Had a nervous breakdown at age 27

Lost a Congressional race at age 34

Lost a Congressional race at age 36

Lost a Senatorial race at age 45

Answer: Abraham Lincoln

Panel 4.12

7 Optimism and Resilience:

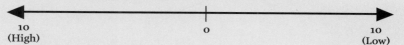

Optimism and Resilience	
High	**Low**
• have a 'can do attitude' • are motivated to continue even when the going gets tough • generally hopeful and positive about life while also remaining realistic	• tend to focus on the negative • see setbacks as permanent • tend to take things personally

Where would you rate yourself on this scale?

```
◄─────────────────────┼─────────────────────►
10                     0                    10
(High)                                    (Low)
```

Is Your Glass Half Full or Half Empty?

Did you know...?
According to psychologist Martin Seligman, author of 'Learned Optimism,' optimists tend to live longer, have fewer illnesses, have lower blood pressure and are ultimately more successful in their lives.

Star Performer

Aung San Suu Kyi

Aung San Suu Kyi has remained an international symbol of heroic and peaceful resistance in the face of oppression in Burma. She has demonstrated great optimism and resilience. Despite being isolated from her family and friends, and under forced 'house arrest' by the Burmese Government for over 6 years, she remains resolute in her fight for democracy for the Burmese people. The inspiration and determination she has shown deservedly earned her the Nobel Peace Prize in 1991.

How Optimists and Pessimists View Setbacks:

Dr. Martin Seligman, leading business psychologist, outlines the difference between how optimists and pessimists explain setbacks to themselves. Unlike optimists, pessimists view setbacks according to the 3 P's: 'Permanent', 'Pervasive' and 'Personal.' This is illustrated below:

For Example: *When you don't get the promotion you want...*

Permanent

❶ **Pessimists view setbacks as <u>permanent</u> while Optimists view setbacks as <u>temporary</u>**

Pessimist: *"I'll never get a job"* versus

Optimist: *"I was unlucky this time."*

Pervasive

❷ **Pessimists view setbacks as <u>pervasive</u> (i.e. all-encompassing) while Optimists view setbacks as <u>specific</u> to that one event**

Pessimist: *"I didn't get the job. It will be the same old story if I go for another interview!"*

Optimist: *"I didn't get the job on this occasion because I didn't prepare well enough."*

Personal

❸ **Pessimists take setbacks <u>personally</u>, while Optimists don't!**

Pessimist: *"They thought I wasn't good enough for the job." or*

Optimist: *"Maybe this job is not for me. Better luck next time!"*

<u>The only difference between the Optimist and the Pessimist is *HOW* they interpret the circumstances around them</u>

◎ Practical Tips:

How did you rate yourself on the optimism and resilience scale? Here are some useful tips which you can work on to develop your optimism and resilience:

→ **Reframe setbacks or problems as 'challenges'**
Remember that each situation can be viewed from different perspectives. The word 'problem' may cause you to feel immobilised, while the word 'solution' will make you feel energised and empowered. It is just like two sides of the same coin!

→ **In the face of setbacks, ask yourself "what can I learn from this?"**
There is no such thing as failure, only feedback! Failure is an essential ingredient for high achievement. In the words of golfer Padraig Harrington: "If you are looking for average, then

try not to make mistakes, but if you are looking to be great, you've got to make loads of mistakes."

→ **Focus on using positive language**
Thoughts, whether positive or negative, tend to attract more of the same. Focus on positive and optimistic thoughts and you will achieve a better outcome. As Jack Canfield of 'The Success Principles' reminds us, "PAY ATTENTION to what you focus on, as it may happen!" (See tools also in Chapter 7)

→ **Develop an attitude of gratitude**
By developing an 'attitude of gratitude' you will begin to appreciate what you have already and immediately put things into a more positive perspective. What are you grateful for today?

Take this time to pause and reflect. Name five things that you are truly grateful for today?

1.
2.
3.
4.
5.

Reframe setbacks as challenges NOT problems

"Accept the things you cannot change, have the courage to change the things you can, and the wisdom to know the difference."

R. Neibuhr

Summary of Chapter 4:

Let's jog your memory of this Chapter!

→ EQ is built on two key pillars: Personal Effectiveness and Interpersonal Effectiveness

→ Great leadership starts with self. To be an effective leader, we must first know, understand and manage ourselves before we can influence others

→ Personal Effectiveness: Involves Knowing and Managing Self and includes:

❶ Self-Awareness: 'tuning in to your internal thoughts, feelings and motivations'

❷ Self-Confidence: 'being self-assured and comfortable in your own skin'

❸ Self-Reliance: 'the buck stops with you!'

❹ Self-Actualisation: 'being self-motivated to achieve your full potential'

❺ Self-Control: 'staying calm and controlled under pressure'

❻ Flexibility: 'being open and responsive to change'

❼ Optimism and Resilience: 'adopting a positive mindset even in the face of setbacks'

→ Self-Awareness is the *cornerstone* of all emotional intelligence from which all the other competencies can be developed

→ Effective leaders strive to achieve a *balance* across all of these competencies.

Interpersonal Effectiveness - Relating to Others

5

Chapter outline
Interpersonal Effectiveness – Relating to Others

"Good leaders make people feel that they're at the very heart of things, not at the periphery."

Warren Bennis

→ **⑧ Empathy:** 'Stepping into someone else's shoes'

→ **⑨ Relationship Skills:** 'Developing and enhancing relationships'

→ **⑩ Assertiveness:** 'Respectfully getting your point across'

Introduction

Building and maintaining good relationships is at the heart of success. By tuning in to and interpreting the emotions of others, we can better communicate, engage and motivate.

In this chapter, we outline the key interpersonal competencies for developing effective communication and relationship-building and provide practical tips for developing each of them.

Highly effective leaders are aware of the need to maintain a sense of balance across all the competencies.

Again in this Chapter, you can use the TACT© approach from Chapter One to help you improve your interpersonal effectiveness.

❽ Empathy: 'stepping into someone else's shoes'

"Seek first to understand and then to be understood."

Stephen R. Covey

How good are you at tuning in to how others are feeling and letting the other person know that they matter? Do you really listen and pick up what's important to the other person as opposed to just focusing on the content of what they are saying?

"Are you listening or are you just waiting to talk?"

Empathy is the ability to accurately tune in to how others think and feel and being able to hear what is not being said. It is essential for good negotiation, in building and retaining customers as well as handling or diffusing conflict. It enables you to see the world from the other person's point of view and understand fully what is important to them.

Great leaders manage their employees with *'tough empathy'* (Goffe and Jones, 2006).

They **empathise passionately yet realistically** with people and **genuinely care** about the work employees do. They can differentiate between what employees need rather than what they want.

Panel 5.1

❽ Empathy:

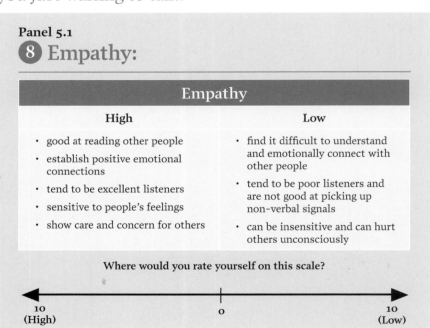

Empathy	
High	**Low**
• good at reading other people • establish positive emotional connections • tend to be excellent listeners • sensitive to people's feelings • show care and concern for others	• find it difficult to understand and emotionally connect with other people • tend to be poor listeners and are not good at picking up non-verbal signals • can be insensitive and can hurt others unconsciously

Where would you rate yourself on this scale?

10 (High) ⟵——————— 0 ———————⟶ 10 (Low)

Star Performer

Nelson Mandela

Former President of South Africa, Nelson Mandela is considered as one of the most charismatic leaders of our time. His diplomacy, mediation and strong empathic skills have been instrumental in developing global relations and reducing conflict.

Scenario:

Sam is conducting an annual performance review with John, one of his top line managers. During their conversation, Sam asks John how everything is going. John replies that everything is 'fine.' However, John is actually unhappy in his job and has been for some time but doesn't feel comfortable telling Sam that this is the case. Sam assumes that everything is fine as he has failed to read John's body language, which sends very different signals. By failing to observe John's non-verbal communication, Sam is in jeopardy of losing one of his best players.

"The most important thing in communication is hearing what isn't said."

Peter Drucker

The 93% Rule:

Albert Mehrabian, the renowned communications researcher, highlighted the importance of meaning in spoken communications as distinct from *words* alone, especially for ambiguous messages. His studies showed that congruence is required between **words, tone of voice and body language.** He found that when communication was ambiguous, words alone only account for 7% of spoken communication. This emphasises the importance of the *'how'* we communicate as opposed to the *'what'* or content.

Therefore, we need to pay attention to the **93% non-verbal** communication, i.e. the body language (visual) and tone of voice (vocal), which we so often overlook. These provide us with the vital clues to the attitude and feelings of others. The 3 V's of communication are shown overleaf:

Panel 5.2

The 3 V's of Communication:

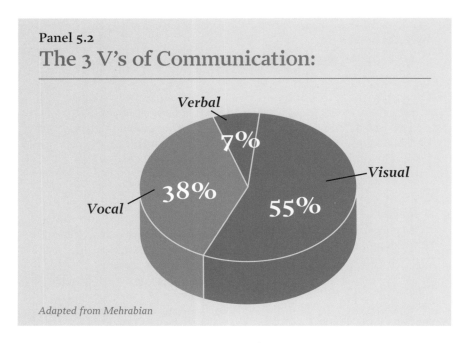

Verbal

7%

Vocal 38%

55% *Visual*

Adapted from Mehrabian

"People will forget what you said, people will forget what you did, but people will never forget how you made them feel."

Maya Angelou

◎ Practical Tips:

How did you rate yourself on the empathy scale? Here are some useful tips which you can work on to develop your level of empathy

→ **Empathy can be developed using the 'HEAR' model**

The HEAR Model

→ H - Have genuine concern and interest in others

→ E - Engage in active listening

→ A - Assess and tune into the non-verbal signals

→ R - Recap and reflect back

→ **Have genuine concern and interest in others**
Show that you are genuinely concerned and interested about the other person and what they are experiencing

→ **Engage in active listening to build understanding and rapport**

- Make eye contact, smile and show your positive intent towards the other person

- Ask open questions to build and enhance what you already know, e.g. *"how do you feel about this?"* can reveal more information and insights about what the person is really thinking and feeling

- Listen twice as much as you speak. Don't interrupt, evaluate or judge

- Show that you are actually listening by nodding and using supportive expressions

→ **Assess and tune into the non-verbal signals!**

- Remember the **'93% rule!'** and the **3 V's of Communication:**
Visuals: body language, facial expressions, eye contact
Vocals: tone of voice, volume, pitch, intonation, and
Verbals: what is actually said

- Just be there with the person. Sometimes silence can be the loudest voice

→ **Recap and reflect back**

- Acknowledge and reflect back your understanding of the situation

- Paraphrase and summarise, for example, *"What I understand from you is...."* *" So what you're saying is...."* *"I can sense that you are frustrated by...."*

❾ Relationship Skills: 'developing and enhancing relationships'

> *"Difficult to manage relationships sabotage more business than anything else - it is not a question of strategy that gets us into trouble; it is a question of emotions."*
>
> John Kotter, Harvard Business School

How good are you at getting on with others? Are you a team player? How much time do you invest in maintaining and building key relationships both at work and at home? Do you take an active interest in developing your people to their potential? How effective are you at managing conflict?

Emotionally-intelligent leaders can navigate social situations skilfully and bring people with them to achieve their goals. They build strong relationships with customers, colleagues and peers.

Panel 5.3

⑨ Relationship Skills:

Relationship Skills	
High	**Low**
• good at building and maintaining relationships • interacts well with others • tolerant of different personalities • demonstrates warmth and openness • readily gets support and commitment from others	• finds it difficult to engage with others • can be ineffective at establishing trust and confidence • can be seen by others as being impersonal and aloof

Where would you rate yourself on this scale?

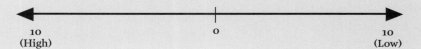

10
(High)

0

10
(Low)

Star Performer

Bill Clinton

Former President Bill Clinton is considered as one of the most charismatic leaders of our time. His people and diplomacy skills have been instrumental in developing global relations and reducing conflict.

Panel 5.4

Building Relationships: Ask yourself 3 questions

→ What percentage of your people do you speak to every day?

→ When was the last time you asked a member of staff about something that was important to them?

→ Do you know what interests your staff members outside work?

◎ Practical Tips:

How did you rate yourself on the relationships skills scale? Here are some useful tips which you can work on to develop your relationship skills

→ **Bring out the best in others**

- Take an active interest in your team and make them feel appreciated through small gestures

- Involve and empower them so that they can shine and develop

- Treat them like winners and they will behave that way *(Pygmalion Effect)*

- Create building blocks for their success through ongoing development of their skills and expertise

---

The Pygmalion Effect

Research indicates that the greater the positive expectation you have of others, the better they perform - a self-fulfilling prophesy!

When Eliza Dolittle was treated like a lady, she then started to behave like one! Similarly, if you treat your people like winners, then they are more likely to behave that way!

→ **Develop tolerance and respect for differences**

- Respect that everyone is different and all have a valuable contribution to bring to the table

- Find ways of acknowledging the benefits of diversity

- Never make assumptions about people

→ **Treat others as you would like to be treated**
Basic as it seems, this age-old proverb rings true every time!

→ **Model excellent communicators**
Observe and model excellent communicators, i.e. colleagues you admire or world-class role models, such as Nelson Mandela or J. F. Kennedy. Take note of how they communicate with others. Observe their posture, gestures, voice and eye contact. How do they hold themselves physically?

→ **Smile!**
Smiling is contagious and creates a feel good factor. As the old saying goes, *'it takes 74 muscles to frown and 12 to smile!'*

→ **Build empathy and rapport**
Refer to the previous competency 'Empathy'.

❿ Assertiveness: 'respectfully getting your point across'

> "The basic difference between being assertive and being aggressive is how our words and behaviour affect the rights and well being of others."
>
> Sharon Anthony Bower, Author

Can you express your feelings thoughts and beliefs openly even when someone disagrees with your point of view? How comfortable are you at giving bad news, or saying 'no' in a way that your colleagues still feel valued? How good are you at standing up for your rights?

Emotionally-intelligent leaders can express their feelings, beliefs and thoughts openly and defend their rights in a respectful manner. Assertiveness is the ability to maintain the right balance between your own needs and other people's needs. It empowers us and is closely associated with a high level of self-confidence and independence.

Panel 5.5

❿ Assertiveness:

Assertiveness	
High	**Low**
• communicates in a straightforward and honest manner	• has difficulty in presenting their opinions/ideas openly to others
• not afraid to voice their opinion even if the majority disagree	• finds it difficult to say 'no' and can become overwhelmed as a result
• not afraid to make unpopular decisions if they feel they are making the 'right' decision	• tends to avoid making unpopular decisions and tend to avoid conflict at all costs
• can say 'no' in a proactive way without offending others	

Where would you rate yourself on this scale?

◄─────────────────────┼─────────────────────►

10
(High)   0   10
(Low)

Star Performer

Martin Luther King

Dr. Martin Luther King stood up for what he believed in and was not afraid to proactively fight for his cause in an assertive and non-threatening manner. He brought together the conscience of the nation and re-focused its priorities in terms of civil rights.

Panel 5.6

Where are YOU on the Assertiveness Scale?

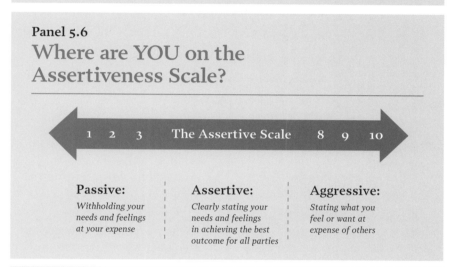

Passive:
Withholding your needs and feelings at your expense

Assertive:
Clearly stating your needs and feelings in achieving the best outcome for all parties

Aggressive:
Stating what you feel or want at expense of others

The importance of 'I' statements:

Part of being assertive involves the ability to appropriately express your needs and feelings in an objective manner. This can be achieved through the use of "I" statements, e.g. *"I feel frustrated when you are late for meetings. I don't like having to keep reminding you,"* as opposed to, *"You're always late for meetings!"*

◎ Practical Tips:

How did you rate yourself on the assertiveness scale?

Here are some useful tips which you can work on to develop your level of assertiveness:

Panel 5.7

Use the ASSERT© model:

A	**Articulate what you want**
S	**Stick to 'I' statements**
S	**Show respect** for the other person
E	**Engage in confident posture**
R	**Rehearse** your ideal outcome
T	**Trust yourself and take action!**

→ **Articulate clearly what you want**
Define clearly what you want to say so that you are more focused and prepared

→ **Stick to 'I' statements**
Avoid getting personal with the other person. Stick to 'I' versus 'You' statements, e.g. *"I feel frustrated when you are late for meetings,"* rather than, *"You are always late for meetings!"*

→ **Show respect for the other person**
Try and understand where the other person is coming from and show them that you respect and understand their position

→ **Engage in confident posture**
Assume an air of confidence before you approach the situation at hand. Reflect this confidence in your body posture. Make direct eye contact and pay attention to your tone of voice and how you project it

→ **Rehearse your ideal outcome**
Visualise a positive outcome in advance of your encounter or situation. Imagine things working out as planned, e.g. see what you see, hear what you hear and feel that feeling of achievement or satisfaction at achieving your desired outcome that respects the views of both parties

→ **Trust yourself and take action!**
Trust your intuition and take action. Be honest in all your dealings. Not to do so will compromise your positive relationships with others in the long-term.

Summary of Chapter 5:

Let's jog your memory of this Chapter!

→ EQ is built on two key pillars: Personal Effectiveness and Interpersonal Effectiveness

→ Building and maintaining relationships is at the heart of success in both our professional and personal lives

→ Interpersonal Effectiveness: Involves relating to others and includes:

8 Empathy: 'stepping into someone else's shoes'

9 Relationship Skills: 'developing and enhancing relationships'

10 Assertiveness: 'respectfully getting your point across'

→ Effective leaders strive to achieve a *balance* across all of these competencies.

Section III
Taking Action to Become a More Effective Leader

In this final section, we provide you with practical tools and exercises to self-assess and develop your EQ leadership skills for lasting results. We also provide tips for staying on track along with additional reading and web resources to help you on your journey!

Your EQ Development Plan and Tips for Staying on Track!

6

Chapter outline
Your EQ Development Plan and Tips for Staying on Track!

→ Key Success Factors for Positive Change!
→ EQ Assessments and Their Benefits
→ Your Five Step EQ Self-Assessment and Development Plan
→ 10 Silver Bullets to Keep You on Track!

Introduction

In this chapter, we provide you with your personal EQ self-assessment and development plan, practical tips for developing your EQ skills and 10 silver bullets to keep you on track!

Key Success Factors for Positive Change!

Research shows that EQ develops with age and life experience. In other words, there is a strong correlation between developed EQ and maturity (BarOn 1980). However, this growth can be accelerated with increased self-awareness and coaching to help you develop and make changes. Once we are aware of the key areas that need development, we can focus on them.

What you focus on GROWS

A large aspect of developing your EQ involves 'unlearning' old habits. We are largely a product of our nature and nurture and we develop values, attitudes and beliefs particular to ourselves. However, as we saw in Chapter 2, the human brain has a high level of 'plasticity' and can develop new neural connections to develop new behaviours, beliefs and mindsets.

Panel 6.1

5 Steps to Positive Change:

1 Open	2 Benefit	3 Focus	4 Implement	5 Find a coach
Be open and committed	See a clear benefit	Stay focused	Implement new habits for 21 days	Partner with a coach, mentor or 'buddy'

→ Be **open** and **committed** to change

→ See the **benefit** associated with the change

→ Stay **focused** on your goal

→ Implement your new **positive habit for at least 21 days**

→ Find a good **mentor, 'buddy' or coach** to partner with

Most training focuses on knowledge and skills, (thinking brain), but deeper changes of attitude and habit, (emotional brain) need to be addressed if sustainable change is going to occur.

The **four stages** in the learning process are highlighted in the learning matrix below:

→ **Unconscious incompetence**
you don't know how to do something. You are unaware and unconcerned

→ **Conscious incompetence**
you begin to learn something new and realise how much you do not know

→ **Conscious competence**
you know how to do something but you must concentrate on it to do it correctly

→ **Unconscious competence**
you are so skilled you do not have to think about it anymore. You operate more on auto-pilot.

Panel 6.2

The Learning Matrix:

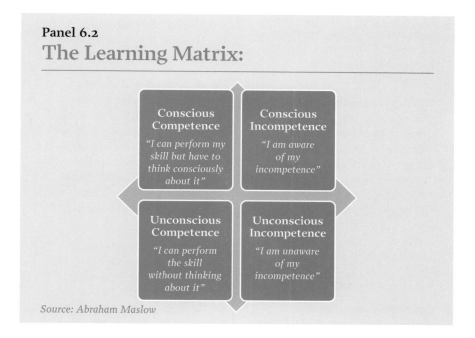

Conscious Competence	Conscious Incompetence
"I can perform my skill but have to think consciously about it"	"I am aware of my incompetence"
Unconscious Competence	Unconscious Incompetence
"I can perform the skill without thinking about it"	"I am unaware of my incompetence"

Source: Abraham Maslow

How can we apply this learning model in the context of EQ?

Think of learning how to ride a bike or drive a car. You would have gone through all of these stages to learn this new skill, from being completely aware of your incompetence, right through to engaging in the task without thinking.

Scenario:

Jane has been given some feedback from a recent performance review that she seems abrupt and sharp with her team members. She demonstrates little or no patience in listening to their concerns or giving them time to air their ideas.

Unconscious incompetence:
Jane is completely unaware of the impact of her behaviour on others. She has always behaved in this manner and doesn't feel the need to change. She fails to realise the impact this is having on the performance of her team. They consistently fail to understand her communications, as she never gives them enough time to clarify any misunderstandings.

Conscious incompetence:
Having been made aware by her supervisor of the impact her behaviour is having on the team, Jane now has a choice to work on her behaviour and focus on her level of empathy and relationship skills. She needs to be more patient, be less prone to angry outbursts and listen attentively to what her team members are saying.

Conscious competence:
Jane has been working with a professional coach over the last three months and is focusing on her listening skills and giving constructive feedback to the team. She has also asked her team members to give her feedback on her behaviour on an ongoing basis, so that she can constantly learn and improve. The level of team productivity and communications has greatly improved.

Unconscious competence:
Over the last few months, following completion of her coaching sessions, Jane is able 'to put herself in the other person's shoes,' as part of her normal behaviour. She is not consciously aware of the need to listen or manage her angry outbursts, as she does it automatically. Jane has now an excellent rapport with all her team members.

EQ Assessments and Their Benefits

There are a number of self assessments available in the market which measure EQ. These will assist you in gaining greater insight into your level of EQ:

→ ECR™ Emotional Capital Report (RocheMartin) specifically designed for the leadership arena

→ Bar-On EQ-i™ Emotional Quotient Inventory (Reuven BarOn)

→ ECI™ Emotional Competency Inventory (Goleman)

→ MSCEIT™ Assessment (Salovey, Mayer and Caruso)

→ EQ Map™.

These assessments provide valuable frameworks for self-awareness and personal development. See Chapter seven for sample of ECR™ leadership summary report.

How can I undergo An EQ Assessment?

To measure and develop EQ skills, you can complete an online assessment which is administered by an EQ accredited coach. A feedback report is supported by three to four coaching sessions to maximise your development and achieve results. The tool can be further supported with 360 degree EQ feedback. For further information, see Chapter 7.

What areas in business can the EQ assessment be used for?

While EQ is only one of a number of measurements used to assist in leadership development, it can support personal and leadership development in many areas as shown below:

Panel 6.3

Valuable Applications

→ recruitment

→ talent management

→ leadership development

→ career planning

→ teambuilding

→ conflict management

→ performance management

→ coaching

Your 5-Step EQ Development Plan

Here is an opportunity to reflect on where you are now. It would be useful to discuss your plan with your manager, a professional coach or mentor who can help you develop your EQ. To refresh your memory of each competency, it may be useful to refer back to Chapter four (Personal Effectiveness) and Chapter five (Interpersonal Effectiveness) and in particular, to see how realistically you rated yourself against each competency.

Panel 6.4

Step 1: Review and rate your EQ competencies

Tick '√' in relevant column: 'Development Opportunity,' Effective Range, 'Strength to Build On' or 'Signature Strength'. Ideally complete this with a trusted colleague, mentor or coach).

Don't forget to check back to Chapters four and five to refresh your memory on what the key skills are and how you self assessed on each skill!

Pillars of EQ	EQ Competence	Development Opportunity	Effective Range	Strength to Build On	Signature Strength
Personal	Self-Awareness				
	Self-Confidence				
	Self-Reliance				

Panel 6.4 (continued)

	Self-Actualisation					
	Self- Control					
	Flexibility					
	Optimism & Resilience					
Interpersonal	Empathy					
	Relationship Skills					
	Assertiveness					

Source: Adapted from the ECR™ (Emotional Capital Report) by Roche Martin

Panel 6.5

Step 2: Identify your top 3 strengths:

Top EQ Competencies:	(a)How do these strengths positively impact you as a leader? (b)How could you further enhance these strengths?
Competency One:	(a) (b)
Competency Two:	(a) (b)
Competency Three:	(a) (b)

Panel 6.6

Step 3: Identify which three competencies you would like to develop and why?

Competency to be Developed:	Why?	What feedback am I getting from my boss, colleagues and peers?
e.g. Empathy	*"I'm not very good at tuning into others and picking up accurate information.* *I feel that if I improve this competency, I will be better able to read my customers and team and get better outcomes from these relationships, i.e. more sales and a more motivated team."*	*My colleagues feel that I do not take their views on board, as I have already made my mind up and don't listen to how they feel about the situation.* *I would have a stronger relationship with my colleagues if they felt I understood where they were coming from.*
1:		
2:		
3:		

Panel 6.7

Step 4: What are the consequences if you decide <u>not</u> to develop these competencies?

Competency to be Developed:	What impact would <u>not</u> developing these competencies have on you as a current and future leader	What impact would <u>not</u> developing these competencies have on my direct reports, colleagues or boss?
e.g. Empathy	"If I don't improve this area, I will miss out on vital information that could really impact the business negatively."	"My current relationship with my direct reports has been poor over the last few months. If I don't take action I will lose their respect as a leader."
1:		
2:		
3:		

Panel 6.8

Step 5: What action are you going to take from today and over the next six months?

Competency to be Developed:	What action are you going to take from today and over the next six months to improve this area:	What tips have I received from my colleagues, coach or mentor on how I can improve?
e.g. Empathy	- Become more self-aware when interacting with others - Listen more actively in conversations and observe non-verbal communication - Consciously make an effort to show concern and interest in other people. - Observe the effects of this behaviour and adapt/revise as appropriate!	"My team have suggested that I take more time to listen to them, to sit down rather than stand all the time when I am talking to them and to be more patient in my dealings with them."
1:		
2:		
3:		

10 Silver Bullets to Keep You on Track!

- **Decide today to improve your level of EQ!**

- **Keep your EQ plan visible and easily accessible at all times**

- **Practise makes perfect!**
  As the old proverb says repetition is the mother of all learning. But its not just about practice! **Perfect** Practise makes perfect. *"We are what we repeatedly do. Excellence, therefore, is not an act but a habit!"* Aristotle

- **Strategically use visual and audio triggers to maintain focus**
  e.g. personalised post-it notes with tips, screensavers, phone reminders, music playlists/ songs to remind you of your goals

- **Schedule a weekly *meeting with yourself***
  Put aside valuable time to reflect and review your progress. Remember if you don't schedule the meetings well in advance, they won't happen! Also if you have a colleague you can trust, look for constructive feedback on how you are doing

- **Immerse yourself in personal development reading/ podcasts/ learning**
  Set time aside to enjoy books, websites and free podcasts which are outlined in the Appendices. If you are commuting, create your own mobile learning centre! This is an ideal opportunity to listen to motivational CD's and books

- **Set aside time to relax and reflect**
  When we do not value ourselves and our energy, we have little left to give to anyone else. Make sure you set aside adequate time daily to recharge and reflect

- **Exercise and eat well**
  'We are what we eat!' as Dr. Gillian Mc Keith tells us. Regular exercise releases endorphins which lift our moods and energise us. When we are healthy, fit and in a good frame of mind we are better able to deal with stress and challenging situations

- **Find a coach/mentor to help you accelerate your development**
  Work with a coach/ mentor who will work with you on a one-to-one basis to help you fast-track your development

- **Enjoy the journey!**
  Enjoy the process of learning. Remember, all the focus will reap positive rewards in both your professional and personal life.

Summary of Chapter 6:

Let's jog your memory of this Chapter!

→ The brain has a high level of 'plasticity' and can form new connections to develop new skills

→ Developing EQ requires a high level of self-awareness, acceptance and commitment to change

→ Remember that what you focus on GROWS!

→ Self Assessments to measure EQ levels can accelerate leadership development, recruitment and assist in developing high potential managers

→ An EQ self-assessment and development plan is a valuable tool for developing your EQ skills

→ 10 silver bullets to keep you on track!

 - Decide today to improve your level of EQ!

 - Keep your plan visible

 - Practise makes perfect

 - Use visual and audio triggers to keep the momentum

 - Set aside a weekly review to 'meet with yourself'

 - Immerse yourself in continuous learning

 - Set aside time to relax and reflect

 - Eat well and exercise

 - Consider using a coach or mentor to accelerate development

 - Enjoy the journey!

Notes

EQ Toolkit & Further Resources

7

Chapter outline
Essential Toolkit & Further Resources

→ **A Sample ECR™ Report:** John Sample
→ **Self-Reliance:** Where is your 'Locus of Control?'
→ **The Wheel of Life:** Taking a Helicopter View of Your Work/Life Balance
→ **Your Values Audit:** Establishing What is Really Important to You
→ **Learning your ABCs:** Reframing Negative Perceptions
→ **ANTS to CATS:** Keeping the Weeds out of Your Garden
→ **Your 'Trophy Room':** A Confidence-boosting Resource
→ **Recommended Reading and Further Resources**

Introduction

In this chapter, we provide you with a useful toolkit and some recommended resources to further support and facilitate your development.

Here you will find six key tools that will help enhance your self-awareness and fast-track your progress!

A Sample ECR™ Report: John Sample

Here, we have chosen a sample of one of a number of EQ tools, the Emotional Capital Report, (ECR™), from Roche Martin, which is specifically tailored to assess EQ skills in the leadership arena.

John is a 30 year-old accountant in an international finance company. His manager regards him as being a very competent and diligent person who has a great deal of integrity.

The company is currently identifying 10 - 15 young managers that are seen to have high potential. John's name has been mentioned on a few occasions by some of the other senior managers as someone with a lot of potential.

By taking the ECR™ self-assessment both John and his manager will gain a better insight into his EQ strengths.

Once he completes the assessment, John will receive an 18 page report and one-to-one feedback from his coach. His manager will then be able to assess his suitability for promotion and to outline the various skills and competencies which he will need to develop in order to make his case more favourable.

The Profile Summary outlined shows a sample of one of the pages of the ECR™ report.

Like all psychometric tools, this tool should only be used as a framework for discussion and development and should not be used in isolation.

If you are interested in taking an ECR™ assessment and receiving a comprehensive ECR development report, refer to 'Resources.'

94

Panel 7.1

ECR Report for: John Sample

ECR - Emotional Captial Report for: John Sample

Self-Awareness / 101

Total Score: 107

| Development Need | Development Opportunity | Effective Range | Strength to Build On | Signature Strength |

Self-Confidence / 113

| Development Need | Development Opportunity | Effective Range | Strength to Build On | Signature Strength |

Self-Reliance / 103

| Development Need | Development Opportunity | Effective Range | Strength to Build On | Signature Strength |

Self-Actualization / 108

| Development Need | Development Opportunity | Effective Range | Strength to Build On | Signature Strength |

Assertiveness / 113

| Development Need | Development Opportunity | Effective Range | Strength to Build On | Signature Strength |

Relationship Skills / 95

| Development Need | Development Opportunity | Effective Range | Strength to Build On | Signature Strength |

Empathy / 83

| Development Need | Development Opportunity | Effective Range | Strength to Build On | Signature Strength |

Self-Control / 112

| Development Need | Development Opportunity | Effective Range | Strength to Build On | Signature Strength |

Flexibility / 106

| Development Need | Development Opportunity | Effective Range | Strength to Build On | Signature Strength |

Optimism / 114

| Development Need | Development Opportunity | Effective Range | Strength to Build On | Signature Strength |

Score Key:

Development Need >80 / Development Opportunity 81-90 /
Effective Range 91-110 / Strength to Build On 111-120 / Signature Strength >121

Source: ECR™Report, RocheMartin.

Evaluating John's ECR™ Report

After examining John's individual ECR™ Report, we can gain some insight into his potential as a leader.

→ **What does John's personal profile suggest about his current levels of Emotional Capital?**

Overall, we can see from the report that John's level of EQ is very positive and is in the effective range, and typical of the general population. However, what the report also tells us, is that he has scope to improve his three lowest competencies - relationship skills, flexibility and particularly empathy

→ **What strengths does John bring to his current role in the organisation?**

John brings great strengths to his current role particularly in the areas of self-confidence and optimism. He has good levels of self-regard and can sustain high levels of motivation. He appears to work well under pressure and maintains a positive outlook in the face of setbacks

→ **What are the challenges John might encounter if he were placed in charge of a large team?**

While John is clearly competent in his job, his interpersonal skills are clearly in need of development if he is to get the best out of his team and progress to a more senior position within the organisation. If he does not

address these areas, he could be in danger of de-motivating his team and not achieving his potential

→ **What are the specific competencies and skills that John needs to develop if he is to step up to leadership positions?**

John needs to develop his interpersonal skills, particularly empathy, and to adopt a more open and flexible approach. He needs to take greater interest in his team and spend more one-to-one time with them. He would be advised to solicit other people's opinions more often and genuinely listen to their point of view before rushing in with his own viewpoints

→ **Considering his age, what might be some medium to long-term development objectives for John's leadership development?**

John clearly needs to invest time in developing his interpersonal competencies, which would enhance his interactions with both his team and all the other stakeholders in the business. To accelerate this process, he could consider attending a communications skills workshop and enlist the support of an executive coach to accelerate the learning process.

Self-Reliance: Where is Your Locus of Control?

Those with a high external locus of control, believe that powerful others, fate, or chance primarily determine events. People with a high internal locus of control, on the other hand, tend to believe that events result primarily from their own behaviour and that they have the power to influence their environment. Complete the following self-assessment to determine your 'locus of control':

Panel 7.2

Self-Reliance: Where is Your 'Locus of Control?'

Read each pair of statements below and circle the statement A or B that you agree with most. Remember there are no right or wrong answers. In some cases, you may agree somewhat with both statements, circle the one with which you agree more.

---

1 A. *Making a lot of money is largely a matter of getting the right breaks*

B. *Promotions are earned through hard work and persistence*

2 A. *There is usually a lot of correlation between how hard I work and the results I get*

B. *Many times the reactions of those assessing me seem haphazard*

3 A. *The number of divorcees suggests that more and more people are not trying to make their marriages work*

B. *Marriage is primarily a gamble*

4 A. *It is silly to think you can really change another person's basic attitudes*

B. *When I am right, I can generally convince others*

5 A. *Getting promoted is really a matter of being a little luckier than the next person*

B. *In our society, a person's future earning power is dependent upon his or her ability*

Panel 7.2 (continued)

6 **A.** *If one knows how to deal with people, they are really quite easily led*

B. *I have little influence over the way other people behave*

7 **A.** *The advances I make are the result of my own efforts; luck has little or nothing to do with it*

B. *Sometimes I feel that I have little to do with the advances I make*

8 **A.** *People like me can change the course of world affairs if we make ourselves heard*

B. *It is only wishful thinking to believe that one can readily influence what happens to me*

9 **A.** *A great deal that happens to me probably is a matter of chance*

B. *I am the master of my life*

10 **A.** *Getting along with people is a skill that must be practiced*

B. *It is almost impossible to figure out how to please some people*

Source: Julian B. Rotter

Panel 7.3

Assessing Your Locus of Control - how did you score?

Scores:

Give yourself one point for each if you chose any of the following answers: 1B, 2A, 3A, 4B, 5B, 6A, 7A, 8A, 9B, 10A.

8-10 **High internal locus of control**

6-7   Moderate locus of control

5   Mixed locus of control

3-4   Moderate external locus of control

1-2 **High external locus of control**

The Wheel of Life: Taking a Helicopter View of Your Work/Life Balance

To be truly fulfilled, one needs to lead a balanced life. When life is busy, or all your energy is focused on a special project, you can find yourself 'off balance,' not paying enough attention to important areas of your life. By regularly taking a 'helicopter view' of your life, you can bring things back into balance.

This is where the 'Wheel of Life' can help. It helps you quickly and graphically identify the areas in your life to which you want to devote more energy.

Panel 7.4

Wheel of Life

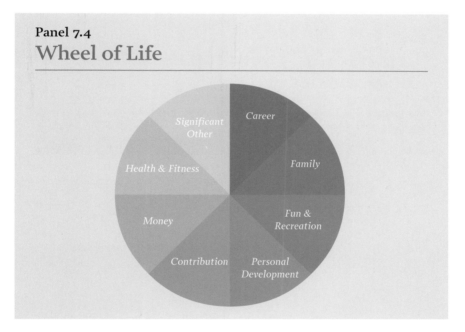

The eight sections of the wheel represent the key areas of your life. Ideally these areas should be in balance just like a wheel.

→ **Step 1:** With the centre of the wheel representing '0' and the outer edge as '10,' rank your level of satisfaction with each area by drawing a line to create a new outer edge

→ **Step 2:** Now join up the marks around the circle. With this new perimeter for the circle, how balanced or 'out of sync' is this wheel? Is it crooked and would it struggle to turn smoothly, or is it perfectly balanced?

→ **Step 3:** Re-plot what you think your ideal satisfaction level would be in each area. A balanced life does not mean getting 10 in each life area. Some areas will need more attention and focus than others at any time

→ **Step 4:** Now you have a visual representation of your current life balance and your ideal life balance. What are the gaps? These are the areas of your life that need attention.

Once you have identified the areas that need attention, what things do you need to start doing to regain balance? In the areas that currently sap your energy and time, what can you stop doing or re-prioritise or delegate to someone else?

Panel 7.5

Step 2: Identify your top three Competencies

Key Areas to Focus on	Goal/Action Plan for Improvement
1: e.g. Health & Fitness	Goal : *'Lose 3 kilos' within two months:* Action: - *Go to gym Mon, Wed and Fri* - *Adopt healthier diet* - *Drink a litre of water per day*
2:	Goal : Action:
3:	Goal : Action:

Your Values Audit: Establishing what is Really Important to You

The very first step on the journey to credible leadership is clarifying your values. Values are very powerful. They are what drive and motivate us. When we are clear on what we stand for, we have much more clarity and control of our lives.

Values are not static or permanent. They evolve over time as we gain more life experiences.

Step 1. From the list of values below, (both work and personal), select 10 with ticks, that are most important to you. Feel free to add any values of your own to this list.

Panel 7.6

What are Your Values?

Honesty		Achievement	
Adventure		Independence	
Challenge		Integrity	
Change and variety		Loyalty	
Creativity		Making a difference	
Excellence		Personal Development	
Democracy		Power	
Family		Quality Relationships	
Financial security		Recognition and status	
Freedom		Teamwork	
Health and Fitness		Wealth	

Add Your Own Values:

Step 2. Once you have...

Once you have reduced the number of values down to 10, imagine that you are only permitted to have five values. What would they be? To what extent are you living your life consistent with these values?

Panel 7.7

Five Values

Most Important Values	List Specific Behaviours consistent with these values that you engage in.
1:	
2	
3:	
4:	
5:	

Learning your ABCs: Reframing Negative Perceptions

Albert Ellis developed the ADCDE model to assist us to adapt and reframe our negative beliefs and hence our behaviour in any given situation. He promoted the idea that it is not what happens to us but how we CHOOSE to respond to situations that is important.

Panel 7.8

An ABCDE Model:

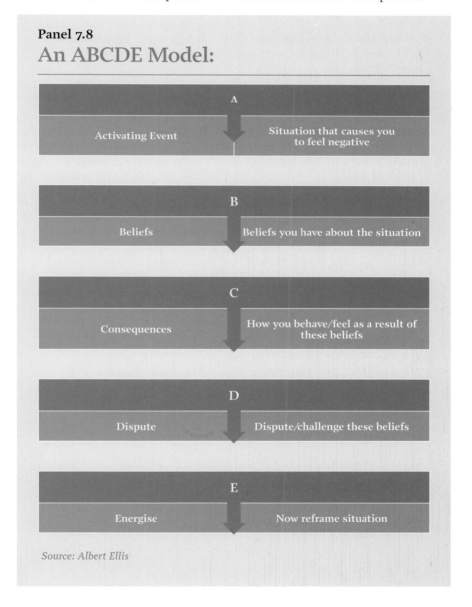

A	
Activating Event	Situation that causes you to feel negative

B	
Beliefs	Beliefs you have about the situation

C	
Consequences	How you behave/feel as a result of these beliefs

D	
Dispute	Dispute/challenge these beliefs

E	
Energise	Now reframe situation

Source: Albert Ellis

→ **A: Activating Event example**

The 'Activating Event' or 'trigger' refers to an event that has actually occurred, a future event that is anticipated or an internal event in your mind such as an image or memory

e.g. *"Our key accounts manager has handed in his resignation and has taken up a new position in another company."*

→ **B: Beliefs**

Your beliefs include your thoughts, self-talk, feelings and meaning you attach to the activating event

e.g. *"We are under serious pressure. We'll never get as good a replacement and our key clients will be upset. I should have seen this coming and spotted that my manager was unhappy."*

→ **C: Consequences**

This refers to the consequences of these beliefs, i.e. how you respond to the situation. This includes your emotions, behaviours and physical sensations associated with these emotions

"I feel under pressure now. I don't think I managed the situation very well. I am sure my boss and team are not impressed. We are coming into our busy season and I have no key accounts person."

→ **D: Dispute/Challenge**

This involves actively disputing, challenging your beliefs about the situation

"Why do I believe this? What proof do I have that this is actually the case? Am I getting things out of proportion?" *"Maybe he was going to leave anyway? If someone asked me for advice about this situation, what would I say?"*

→ **E: Energise for Effective Outcome**

This involves reframing your thinking as a result of challenging beliefs, to achieve a positive outcome

e.g. *"No-one is completely indispensable. Maybe we need new blood anyway. Must get on the case straight away and look at all my options. Keep things in perspective."*

Exercise:

ABCDE Model

Think of a recent setback you encountered or are encountering and try the ABCDE approach:

A Activating Event	
B Beliefs	
C Consequences	
D Dispute/Challenge	
E Energise	

Source: Albert Ellis

"Nothing is either good or bad but thinking makes it so."

William Shakespeare

ANTS to CATS - Keeping the Weeds out of the Garden

According to psychologists, we all have approximately 50,000 thoughts per day. Many of these thoughts relate to what we did/ didn't do in the past, what we are going to do with the future but forgetting about the present moment!

We also have what are known as ANTS or Automatic Negative Thoughts which pop in and out of our heads. These ANTS are unproductive and zap valuable energy, which could be deployed more productively in other areas. The challenge is to become the observer of your thoughts and filter what actually gets in. As the saying goes, 'garbage in, garbage out' so be very selective about where you focus your thoughts and energy.

We also know that whatever we focus on GROWS! If you focus on something negative happening, it is more likely to become a self-fulfilling prophesy!

Think of your mind as a garden. Most gardeners make sure that they keep the weeds out so that the plants and flowers can flourish. And so it is with our thoughts. The objective is to stamp out those ANTS and replace them with CATS or Confidence Affirming Thoughts. Tell yourself that you can do it and you go a long way towards proving yourself right.

While Confidence Affirming Thoughts (CATS) are strong positive statements, it is important that your goals are realistic and based on focused development plans, not just aspirations. CATS can help us rid ourselves of negative self-talk and replaces this negative chatter with positive ideas and concepts.

Panel 7.9

Replace ANTS with CATS

ANTS Automatic Negative Thoughts	CATS Confidence Affirming Thoughts
"I am not that good at my job"	"I am a natural leader and a positive inspiration to others"
"I always dread presentations to the board"	"I am always fully prepared and deliver confident presentations every time"
"I am a poor communicator"	"I communicate with ease and conviction"
"I feel foolish when I make mistakes"	"I am not perfect. I see setbacks as learning opportunities"
"My staff don't feel appreciated"	"I give my staff positive compliments and encouragement at every opportunity"

Your 'Trophy Room' - A Confidence-Boosting Resource

Here is a tool to help you reflect and record your key strengths, talents and achievements over the course of your life to date. It is a powerful tool to reflect on for further developing your self-confidence and help you maximise your natural abilities.

Panel 7.10

Your Trophy Room

List your key achievements in the following areas:

1. Education
-
-
-

2. Career Highlights
-
-
-

3. Sport
-
-
-

4. Other Hobbies & Interests (Music/Art/Drama)
-
-
-

5. Community or Charity work
-
-
-

What Knowledge, Skills, Abilities, Talents or a combination helped you realise these achievements?

Panel 7.10 (continued)

What have others i.e. parents, teachers, lecturers, managers, coaches, mentors, peers or friends recognised as your key achievements and why?

From your self-reflection and what others think, what are your top five strengths?

-
-
-
-
-

What achievement are you are most proud of and why?

When you reflect on highlights of your life, what songs played a significant role and created momentum and inspiration for you? What would be your ideal 'playlist' for motivating YOU?

Favourite Playlist:

- Music for sporting pastimes:
- Music for relaxation:
- Music to inspire me:
- Music to energise me:

Recommended Reading and Further Resources

Recommended Reading:

Albrecht, K. (2006):
Social Intelligence

Bennis, W. (1998):
On Becoming a Leader

Caruso, D. and Salovey, P. (2004):
The Emotionally-Intelligent Manager

Collins, J. (2001):
Good to Great

Cooper, R. and Sawaf, A. (1998):
Executive EQ - Emotional Intelligence

Covey, S. R. (1992):
*The 7 Habits of Highly
Effective People*

Goleman, D. (1995):
Emotional Intelligence

Goffee, R. and Jones, G. (2006):
Why Should Anyone be Led by You?

Hill, D. (2007):
*Leveraging Emotions for
Business Success*

Kouzes M. & Posner, L. (2007):
The Leadership Challenge

Newman, M. (2007):
*Emotional Capitalists -
The New Leaders*

Pink, D. H. (2005):
*A Whole New Mind - Why
Right-Brainers will Rule the Future*

Seligman, M. (2006):
*Learned Optimism - How to Change
your Mind and Your Life*

Sharma, R. (2006):
The Greatness Guide

Stein, S. J. and Book, H. E. (2000):
The EQ Edge

Websites and Podcasts:

www.managementbriefs.com

www.rochemartin.com

www.eiconsortium.com

www.thesuccessprincipals.com

www.authentichappiness.com

You can check out and download various free podcasts on leadership and EQ on iTunes

Further Information:

For further information on EQ Assessments, Leadership Development and Coaching, contact Daire at: daire@ ManagementBriefs.com, or Deirdre at: deirdre@ManagementBriefs.com or log on to www.ManagementBriefs.com.

Notes

Notes

Notes

Notes

Notes

Notes

Notes

Notes

Further publications in 2011 and 2012

- → Managing Reward
- → Handling Discipline - *Best Practice*
- → Managing Diversity
- → Negotiating Skills
- → Burnout
- → Coaching Skills
- → Life Balance
- → Conflict Resolution
- → Influencing Skills
- → Mediation Skills
- → Assertiveness and Self-Esteem
- → Strategic Issue Communications
- → Personal Development
- → Innovation
- → Compliance
- → Strategy Development and Implementation
- → Leadership and Strategic Change
- → Managing with Impact - *Focusing on Performance through People*
- → Strategic Marketing
- → Entrepreneurial Skills
- → Managing Attendance at Work
- → Employee Relations
- → Improving your Writing Skills
- → Organisation Development/ Training
- → Change Management
- → Organisation Design
- → Energy Management
- → International Marketing
- → Governance in Today's Corporate World
- → Customer Relationship Management
- → Building Commitment to Quality
- → Understanding Finance
- → PR Skills for Managers
- → Logistics and Supply Chain
- → Dealing with Difficult People
- → Effective Meetings
- → Communication Skills
- → Facilitation Skills
- → Managing Upwards
- → Giving and Receiving Feedback
- → Consumer Behaviour
- → Delegation and Empowerment
- → Basic Economics for Managers
- → Finance for non Financial Executives
- → Business Forecasting
- → The Marketing of Services

Management Briefs
Essential Insights for Busy Managers

Our list of books already published includes:

→ Be Interview-Wise: *How to Prepare for and Manage* <u>*Your*</u> *Interviews*
  Brian McIvor

→ HR for Line Managers: *Best Practice*
  Frank Scott-Lennon & Conor Hannaway

→ Bullying & Harassment: *Values and Best Practice Responses*
  Frank Scott-Lennon & Margaret Considine

→ Career Detection: *Finding and Managing Your Career*
  Brian McIvor

→ Impactful Presentations: *Best Practice Skills*
  Yvonne Farrell

→ Project Management: *A Practical Guide*
  Dermot Duff & John Quilliam

→ Marketing Skills: *A Practical Guide*
  Garry Hynes & Ronan Morris

→ Performance Management: *Developing People and Performance*
  Frank Scott-Lennon & Fergus Barry

→ Proven Selling Skills: *For Winners*
  Ronan McNamara

→ Redundancy: *A Development Opportunity for You!*
  Frank Scott-Lennon, Fergus Barry & Brian McIvor

→ Safety Matters!: *A Guide to Health & Safety at Work*
  Adrian Flynn & John Shaw of Phoenix Safety

→ Time Matters: *Making the Most of Your Day*
  Julia Rowan

→ Emotional Intelligence (EQ): *A Leadership Imperative!*
  Daire Coffey & Deirdre Murray